# ABORTION
Breaking the Silence
in the Church

Also by Jonathan Jeffes:

What Happens After an Abortion?
Unplanned Pregnancy: Talking with Teenagers (Booklet)

# ABORTION
## Breaking the Silence in the Church

### JONATHAN JEFFES

*LP* LEAN PRESS LIMITED

**LP** LEAN PRESS LIMITED

First published in Great Britain in 2013 by Lean Press Limited

© Jonathan Jeffes 2013

The right of Jonathan Jeffes to be identified as the Author of the Work has been asserted by him in accordance with the Copyright, Designs and Patents Act, 1988.

All rights reserved. No part of this publication may be reproduced, stored in a retrieval system, or transmitted in any form or by any means without the prior written permission of the publisher, nor be otherwise circulated in any form or binding or cover other that in which it is published and without a similar condition being imposed on the subsequent purchaser.

ISBN: 978-0-9576513-1-9

Scripture quotations are from
THE HOLY BIBLE, NEW INTERNATIONAL VERSION®,
NIV® Copyright © 1973, 1978, 1984, 2011 by Biblica, Inc.™
Used by permission. All rights reserved worldwide.

Lean Press Limited
PO Box 58
26 The Hornet
Chichester
PO19 7BB

Email: info@leanpress.co.uk

Design and typesetting by Andy Ashdown Design
www.andyashdowndesign.co.uk

Cover image: © Kevin Carden | Dreamstime.com

Manufactured in Great Britain by Halcyon

Dedicated to Francesca
with all my love and deep gratitude
for your support and encouragement
in this project over the years.

# Contents

| | | |
|---|---|---|
| Introduction | | 9 |
| Chapter 1 | Why the silence in the church? | 15 |
| Chapter 2 | What the silence is hiding | 25 |
| Chapter 3 | What happens after an abortion? | 35 |
| Chapter 4 | Introducing effective change in the church | 47 |
| Chapter 5 | Shaping an effective personal view | 59 |
| Chapter 6 | How to win friends and influence people when speaking about abortion in a church setting | 69 |
| Chapter 7 | Pastoral care in the local church | 89 |
| Chapter 8 | Breaking the silence in the church | 99 |
| Appendix I | Rape and abortion | 109 |
| Appendix II | Disability, pre-natal screening and abortion | 117 |
| Appendix III | Are there psychological risks to an abortion? | 125 |
| Acknowledgements | | 131 |

# Introduction

## Why should Christians engage with the subject of abortion?

A powerful silence has grown up around the subject of abortion. This book has been written for Christians, church leaders and those with pastoral or counselling responsibilities in churches. It aims to help them understand why the silence is there, reveal what the silence is hiding and point to ways that it can be broken effectively, but with humility, compassion and understanding.

Perhaps a good place to start is by asking: why should Christians and church leaders be interested in the subject of abortion, why should this topic be a priority?

Here is one simple fact, taken from the Office for National Statistics 2010 report: **34% of all women in the United Kingdom will experience at least one abortion in their lifetime.**[1] Or as a report from The Royal College of Obstetricians and Gynecologists recognised:

> "At least one third of women will have had an abortion by the time they reach the age of 45 years."[2]

The truth is that a pandemic of abortion is taking place all around us at every level of our society, mostly in secrecy and complete silence. The sheer scale of what is happening means that abortion has the potential to touch the lives of each one of us. Do not be fooled by the silence into thinking it is not a problem for Christians or a problem in our churches. Rather, Christians desperately need to have an informed understanding of what is going on, and to have useful points of reference for engaging with the subject.

Twenty years ago I trained to become a crisis pregnancy counsellor. Having become involved in this work in central London, the need to provide counselling for women (and men) who approached us for help with issues pertaining to a past abortion became apparent. Together with Nicky-Sue Leonard, I established a post-abortion recovery course, which has run regularly since 1993. Over the years our counselling team has talked with a wide variety of people of different ages and diverse backgrounds. In total we have counselled over 200 women and around 30 men, most of whom experienced abortion in their early 20s (though some when they were teenagers; some later in life). The reasons why some men and women maintain a strong connection with a past abortion will be explained later in the book.

As our post-abortion work became known, we were occasionally asked to speak to small groups in different churches. I noticed that the experience we shared from our groups seemed to engage a church audience in a way that traditional teaching on abortion did not. This book has therefore been written to reflect some of our experience and offer a practical guide for leaders.

There is a pressing need to engage with the issue of abortion. As I will show, the current silence in the church leaves Christians

## INTRODUCTION

vulnerable to the fallout of an unplanned pregnancy, and also prevents Christians who have had an abortion from reconciling their experience with their faith. This in turn creates unseen tension and prevents the subject being discussed openly.

It seems to me that when it comes to abortion, Christians can find it difficult to believe that there is a problem in their own church. There can be an assumption that it is only something that happens elsewhere, to other people. However, I noticed that sometimes when visiting other churches, if people hear of our work, individuals regularly come to talk with me about their past abortions, even in churches where leaders say there is not a problem.

I have had many discussions with church leaders who assure me that they have never come across the issue of abortion in their own congregations, but the truth is that often people from those churches end up on our post-abortion healing course. We estimate that around half of those attending our course had their abortions before they became a Christian, and about half when they already had a faith, so we believe that there is a widespread culture of secret abortion in the church today. My experience has been that if you go looking for it, you will find it. If you start talking about it with compassion and understanding, the issue will be revealed.

To my knowledge, no one has undertaken a study to assess how widespread abortion is among Christians in the UK. But in America, where the profile of those going for abortions closely mirrors our own, many thorough surveys show that the abortion rate amongst Christians of all denominations and beliefs closely follows the national trend. John Ensor, a pastor in America who conducted a survey in his church said, "I was shocked to find that fully 30% of women in my own church congregation were post-aborted."[3] Just looking at the similarity of the statistics must mean that abortion is a much bigger problem in the UK church than is currently realised.

I have called this book "Breaking the Silence" because that is what I wish to achieve. But I want to do so in a quiet, gentle manner that will equip Christians to respond to the issue with the Christian strengths of compassion and pastoral care, rather than with judgment and condemnation. I am not part of a campaign and I am not seeking to make abortion illegal; rather, my hope is to inspire Christians to have the nerve to tackle a difficult subject with courage and imagination, but also with humility, compassion and understanding.

Therefore, this book includes:

- An overview of traditional Christian teaching;
- An analysis of why this teaching has become largely ineffective and given rise to an uncomfortable silence in the church;
- A suggested simple strategy for change;
- Practical advice to support change including guidance on speaking about abortion in a church setting, and guidance on handling it as a pastoral issue.

I appreciate that modern church leaders are busy people, and I have given careful thought to making this book as brief and practical as possible.

## INTRODUCTION

I believe that with a few small changes Christians could be empowered to have something useful to say to their friends, within their families and in their local communities on the issue of abortion.

[The word 'pastoral' can have a slightly different meaning according to different Christian traditions. In this book the word 'pastoral' is intended to convey a counselling or spiritual guidance context, rather than a communal presence or evangelistic context.]

Jonathan Jeffes

# Chapter 1

## Why the silence in the church?

*In this chapter the section on the Bible and Christian tradition was written by the Reverend Sean Doherty, ethics tutor at St Mellitus Theological College, London.*

The speed at which abortion was legalised in the 1960s seemed to catch many political and church leaders off-guard. Christians have since sought to make sense of this situation and understand how it was that abortion became so rapidly and widely accepted. Perhaps the best place to start is by reviewing traditional church teaching on the subject and exploring how Christians have responded to the issue – both historically and since it was legalised.

## Traditional church teaching – what does the Bible say about abortion?

Scripture makes no specific mention of abortion. If we (mis)treat the Bible as if it were an exhaustive rulebook, we might therefore assume that it does not say anything about abortion, either for or against. Or we might go to the other extreme, quoting a text such as,

"You shall not murder" (Exodus 20:13) as if it settles the matter all by itself. Yet how are we to tell whether abortion falls into such a category or not? Clearly a more careful reading of the overall witness of Scripture is required.

In the creation narratives of Genesis 1 and 2, we find that humans are not disembodied spirits, but physical, bodily creatures, created from the dust of the earth. This physical life is part of what is described as "very good" (Genesis 1:31). Perhaps most fundamentally, we are told that humanity is made in God's image. Therefore, we should resist separating off the 'higher' human functions such as the capacity to think, feel or choose. These things are not what make us human or what make us precious. Our preciousness is ours by the fact that we are made by God and bear his image. The value of human bodily life is therefore *intrinsic*: it is given to us as a gift, rather than being earned or lost by our efforts and capacities.

A person with severe mental and physical disabilities who cannot move, choose or reason is still fully human and precious as a person. Similarly, an embryo is a person, not because of any acquired ability or features it possesses, but because it has been given the gift of human bodily life and is therefore made in the image of God. We cannot pinpoint a time that life begins, other than when human bodily life begins. An embryo may lack sentience, rationality and autonomy, but it is a separate physical, living human being from the moment of its conception (that is, the moment at which a sperm fertilises an egg). This is what makes it precious to God, and this is what makes its deliberate destruction prohibited, in nearly all circumstances.[4]

The creation of humanity in God's image is the reason Scripture gives for its prohibition on taking innocent life.[5] In Genesis 9:6, God explicitly prohibits the shedding of human blood *because* humanity is made in the image of God. The prohibition on murder found in the Ten Commandments is therefore not some arbitrary edict that can be taken in isolation. Rather, it is a summary of how we should act, given the way that Scripture describes bodily human life as precious and made in the image of God.

Seeing the sixth commandment in this light helps to make sense of the absolute and non-negotiable way in which it is expressed. It does not invite us to weigh up the lesser of two evils or to produce the best possible outcome in tragic circumstances.[6] It summons us to simple obedience in trust that God wants what is best for his creatures and that he alone can redeem the tragedy of human fallenness.

The goodness of human bodily life is of course supremely reaffirmed in the incarnation and resurrection of Jesus Christ. God himself stoops to take on our bodily nature with all its limitations and imperfections, and he hallows it by ascending bodily to heaven. The account of the incarnation in Luke's gospel is particularly illuminating, since it gives us a helpful pointer on the question of when human life begins: "You will conceive," says Gabriel to Mary, "and give birth to a son, and you are to call him Jesus" (Luke 1:31).

It is certainly stretching the point to read this as a proof that life begins at the moment of conception, since it is doubtful that the Greek here carries the connotation of fertilisation. But it does cohere with the wider biblical witness to the value of life in the womb, and the presence and involvement of God in its development. Perhaps the most famous instance is the beautiful description in Psalm 139:13–14:

> "For you created my inmost being;
> You knit me together in my mother's womb.
> I praise you because I am fearfully and wonderfully made."

Other texts are even more radical. Jeremiah 1:4–5 refers to God's knowledge and setting apart of the prophet even *before* he had been "formed in the womb". Job curses the very night he was conceived (Job 3:3). Of course, these texts do not say absolutely and with crystal clarity when life begins but, as John Stott puts it, they do point to the *continuity* between the personal identity of the fully developed adult, and the embryo or foetus as it grows in the womb.[7]

Stott therefore concludes that, according to Scripture, "The foetus is neither a growth in the mother's body, nor even a potential human being, but already a human being who, though not yet mature, has the potentiality of growing into the fullness of the individual humanity he already possesses."[8]

So, at the very least, we can say that Scripture reveals that the beginning of human life is very early on in pregnancy. We have not found direct 'proof' that human life begins at conception, because that is the moment at which it physically begins, but what we *have* found certainly points, at the very least, in this direction.

The absence of absolute proof on this point need not deter us from recognising that the deliberate destruction of life from the moment of fertilisation is wrong in nearly all circumstances because the development of the embryo is gradual. The fact is that there is no objective point other than conception at which we can say that a human life, which did not exist before that moment, has come into existence. As human life is so precious, and its destruction so terrible, unless we have proof that embryos are not people, we are obliged to treat them as such.

There is one final point to draw from our exploration of the biblical creation stories, and that is their emphasis on humans as communal and relational creatures. Genesis 1 notes that it is *together* that men and women are created in the image of God (1:27). And Genesis 2:18 shows us that it is "not good" for Adam to be alone (Genesis 2:18). Humans are not created to live in isolation; we were created to live in relationship with others. So the vulnerability and absolute dependence of an embryo upon its mother does not disqualify it from being protected and cherished as much as any developed human life. Quite the opposite: its vulnerability and need for protection is a further indication of its humanity.

Let us summarise our conclusions, drawn from this biblical exploration.

First, as is well known, Scripture prohibits the destruction of innocent life.

Second, it does so because humans are made in God's image and are precious to him.

Third, what makes us human is not whether we are rational, sentient or conscious, but whether we are *physically* alive. This means that life begins at the moment at which it begins *physically*, that is, conception (fertilisation). This is corroborated by the way in which the Bible indicates that God is intimately involved and concerned with human life from a very early stage of its development in the womb, and that from a very early stage this life is identified as the same person who will eventually be born.

Fourth, because the destruction of innocent human life is such a serious matter, even those who are not convinced that human life begins at conception should be encouraged to err on the side of caution and act *as if* it does, unless they can prove otherwise beyond all reasonable doubt.

It seems to me, therefore, that from an analysis of Scripture the following acts are ruled out:

- Abortion because the pregnancy is unwanted;
- Abortion because the child will be disabled;
- Tests such as amniocentesis, which carry a risk and offer no medical benefit to the child;
- Forms of contraception that function by inhibiting implantation (i.e. intrauterine devices and some forms of the pill).

## Christian tradition and abortion

We have seen that, despite the absence of direct reference to abortion in the Bible, a very clear position with respect to abortion emerges from it, as is seen in the teaching of the Christian tradition. The earliest direct reference in church history to abortion is contained in *The Didache* (late first/early second century), which states, "You shall not kill the child in the womb or cause a new born infant to perish".[9]

In the second century, the Christian philosopher Athenagoras wrote, "We say to those women who use drugs to bring on abortion that they commit murder and will have to give an account to God for the abortion."[10] The great theologians from the Middle Ages, through the

Reformation and on to modernity have all reaffirmed this position, from Augustine to Calvin, and from Bonhoeffer to Karl Barth.

The great theological traditions and Christian denominations are similarly united behind the traditional doctrine that abortion is unacceptable leaving aside operations to save a mother's life, which some do not see as abortion as the ending of the baby's life is not the intention of the operation. The Catechism of the Catholic Church (paragraph 2270) teaches:

> "Human life must be respected and protected absolutely from the moment of conception. From the first moment of his existence, a human being must be recognised as having the rights of a person, among which is the inviolable right of every innocent being to life."

This position was most recently reaffirmed in the papal encyclical *Evangelium Vitae* (Gospel of Life), in which John Paul II declared that the Church's teaching on abortion "is unchanged and unchangeable".

Also of interest is the Church of England's position on abortion, as expressed in the 1980 statement of the Church of England's Board of Social Responsibility, which says, "In the light of our conviction that the foetus has the right to live and develop as a member of the human family, we see abortion, the termination of that life by the act of man, as a great moral evil. We do not believe that the right to life, as a right pertaining to persons, admits no exceptions whatsoever; but the right of the innocent to life admits surely of few exceptions indeed."

The "few exceptions" were stated in the 1983 General Synod resolution as: "situations where continuance of the pregnancy threatens the life of the mother." The resolution concluded, "All life, including life developing in the womb, is created by God in his own image and is, therefore, to be nurtured, supported and protected."

Many major Christian denominations in Britain today (including Catholics, Anglicans, Presbyterian, Baptists, Methodists, Pentecostal and some independent churches) have policies and articles that declare that abortion is either undesirable or unacceptable, or both.

## Recent times

In spite of Christian objections, abortion was legalised in 1967 and organisations with strong Christian support such as the Society for the Protection of Unborn Children (SPUC) and LIFE have since sought to reverse this decision, with regular campaigns seeking to make abortion illegal. Contentious groups such as Operation Rescue undertake well-publicised action such as picketing abortion clinics and holding demonstrations. The charity 'Christian Action Research and Education' (CARE) was established in the UK for the promotion of the Christian perspective on life issues, and responded to the issue of abortion by establishing a network of crisis pregnancy centres and by developing education programmes addressing issues of sex and relationships. This department of CARE, known as CareConfidential, has recently become a separate charity, as the work has steadily grown and is today the only Christian organisation with a national presence. Recently *40 Days for Life* has become a popular movement of prayer and peaceful public vigils.

Although the official position of most major church denominations remains that abortion is either undesirable or unacceptable, at least outside the context of saving a mother's life, in recent times there has been an increasingly widespread acceptance of abortion at all levels of society, including among Christians.

A 2010 major YouGov poll indicated that even 70% of Catholics in the UK now think a woman should be able to choose an abortion, a position that would have been unthinkable even a few years ago.[11] As a result of this increasing acceptance, a gap has opened up between most church leaders, who hold traditional values, and the majority of their congregations who do not. Into this gap a powerful silence has grown up around abortion which has become a sensitive and contentious subject. At present, any discussion or even use of the word "abortion" in a church setting has the potential to anger or upset people, perhaps due to the unattractive way the arguments are sometimes presented and can thus appear judgmental and bigoted to a modern audience.

As a result, many Christians occupy a sort of neutral ground that neither supports abortion, nor condemns it. Some would sum up their attitude by saying, "I would not have an abortion myself, but I would not judge someone who did." Trying to reconcile the position that abortion is neither right nor wrong results in a strong desire to avoid the subject altogether. Any mention of abortion requires making a value judgment, which may involve judging others.

As the desire to avoid being judgmental is paramount, abortion is viewed as a subject that is too sensitive, and almost sinful, to talk about in a Christian context. An interesting dynamic we observed on our post-abortion courses was that participants often told us they felt happier talking about abortion with their non-Christian friends, than with their Christian friends.

Many Christians believe that the silence and refusal to engage with the subject is compassionate, but in reality the silence simply covers up the problem so that church leaders find it difficult to see and understand it in their own congregations. The silence stops people seeking help for a past abortion and leaves Christians vulnerable to abortion. It also means that extreme groups remain unchallenged.

Therefore, a new model of engagement with the issue of abortion is needed. This will enable the subject to be accessible to a new generation of Christians, and enable the church to assert its traditional position in a way that can be heard, thus leading people away from abortion.

I believe that, by engaging with the issue, individuals could do much to avoid abortion in their own lives, their own families and within their church communities. If the church is encouraged to respond compassionately and sensitively to abortion, Christians could begin to influence the surrounding culture and play to traditional strengths of love and pastoral care. Christians could begin to make a huge difference.

# Chapter 2

## What the silence is hiding

Abortion may be a difficult subject to raise within the church, but a powerful silence also surrounds it outside the church – a silence that hides what is really happening. When I raise the subject of abortion with others, the immediate response often centres on concern for teenagers. It is true that the teenage pregnancy rate in the UK is high; every year approximately 35,000 of those aged under 18 experience an unplanned pregnancy.[12] Of those, approximately 16,000 will have an abortion, the remainder will give birth.[13] Although these figures seem large, they actually represent a small percentage of the general population aged 15–17. Around 3.5% of under 18s will thus experience an unplanned pregnancy, and 1.7% of under 18s will experience an abortion.

However, the greatest problem does not lie with the teenage pregnancy rate. If these figures seem alarming, they are nothing compared with what is happening in the general population aged over 18. On an unimaginable scale, a pandemic of abortion is washing through virtually every level of our society.

The truth is this: overall, a woman growing up in Britain today:

- Will have a 6% chance of having an abortion by the time she reaches her 20th birthday;[14]
- A 17% chance by the time she reaches 25.[15]

Also:

- 34% of all British women will experience one or more abortions in their lifetime;[16]
- One third of all abortions are repeat procedures, therefore 10% of all British women will experience more than one abortion.[17]

As we will see, unintended pregnancy is no respecter of social class, education or background in the UK. It takes place across all sections of society. Therefore, it is important that we engage with, and understand, abortion; no matter who we are or where we are from, it could affect us – either personally or in the lives of our family and friends.

Perhaps the best starting point in beginning to understand what is going on is to consider typical profiles of those who have an abortion, and understand why they get unintentionally pregnant, why they choose abortion, and what happens to them afterwards.

## Who has an abortion?

The majority of people who have abortions are aged between 20 and 25, however this is the only real differential. It seems that neither social class, income bracket nor, sometimes, even faith makes a difference. As revealed in the official Department of Health statistics for abortion in England and Wales,[18] there are minor variations in the demographics, but essentially an unemployed person living in an area of urban deprivation is just about as likely to have an abortion as a wealthy person living in an area of affluence.

Although married couples are much less likely to choose abortion, 16% of those who had an abortion in 2010 were married.[19] The overwhelming majority (more than 97%) of people choose abortion for personal reasons; fewer than 1% of abortions are carried out due to medical conditions or disabilities, such as Down's Syndrome.[20] Although rape is a terrible act in our society and official statistics for the number of abortions due to rape are, to my knowledge, not available, it is estimated that the numbers of pregnancies and subsequent abortions due to rape are still mercifully small at less than 1–2%. (See Appendix I for further information on the issue of rape and abortion.)

## Why do women get pregnant if they do not want to be?

Why do so many of our population experience an unintended pregnancy followed by an abortion? Is it ignorance, bad luck or something else?

Studies show that a substantial majority (one authoritative study showed 62%[21], another 86%[22]) of people presenting themselves for an abortion believed that they were using effective contraception. Other findings show that nearly 100% of people having an abortion knew about contraception at the time of conception and probably had access to it. Furthermore, they had almost certainly used some form of contraceptive method in the past.[23]

It is therefore important to understand that, contrary to popular assumption, it is not generally a lack of knowledge about contraception that causes an unintended pregnancy resulting in an abortion.

The claim "Safe Sex Prevents Pregnancy" is often made. However, the evidence seems to suggest otherwise. For example, according to the latest research from the US, if twelve women take oral contraceptives over the course of one year, one will fall pregnant. For condoms the odds are closer to one in six.[24]

Today, most people in a sexual relationship believe that with a good knowledge of (and access to) contraception, they will not experience pregnancy or 'need' an abortion. In fact, anyone intending to control their fertility using contraception could be at risk of unintended pregnancy due to a complex mix of factors.

If contraception were to be used in a controlled setting, or in a laboratory experiment, some methods would be nearly 100% effective.[25] Of course, the inconvenient truth is that we do not live in a laboratory, and we do not live in controlled conditions – life gets in the way. In many ways, contraception runs contrary to human nature.

Our experience with the post-abortion recovery course has taught us that the relationship between contraceptive intention and pregnancy can be extremely complex. Over the years, we have heard some seemingly irrational or illogical stories from otherwise highly controlled and methodical individuals. The fact of the matter is that human beings are neither entirely rational, nor entirely consistent. As C.S. Lewis put it: "Their [human beings'] nearest approach to constancy is undulation – the repeated return to a level from which they repeatedly fall back – a series of troughs and peaks."[26]

Out of our deepest instincts to be loved and to express love comes, for nearly all of us, the desire to find a partner and have children – the desire to reproduce. This instinct is so powerful that it can drive strong subconscious desires and behaviours. Some women will get pregnant deliberately in an attempt to resolve relationship issues, but many others (sometimes with the encouragement or collusion of the man involved), will become pregnant due to a complex mix of passion, impulse, desire, frustration, circumstances and sometimes with a little bit of irrationality or in a moment of madness.

From the outside, an observer might describe such behaviour as deliberate or intentional, but men and women who have been in this position generally see it as an accident, or in terms of being overtaken by events or circumstances beyond their control. The increasing use of the phrase, "I fell pregnant" seems to reflect a developing, unconscious awareness that we do not control our fertility, rather that it is something that happens to us regardless of our contraceptive choices.

I am not suggesting that women who have abortions get pregnant deliberately, but from what people on our courses tell us, there can be a degree of intentionality, albeit perhaps to a very small degree, from both women and men with *some* unintended pregnancies.

I would suggest that it is the unrealistic expectation that we can control our own fertility that drives the high abortion rate. Contraception may give us partial control over our fertility, but it does not always give us absolute control over it in practice. For nearly half the population, contraception will not prevent pregnancy[27], and one third of our female population will experience at least one abortion. These are the real facts of life.

## Why do people choose abortion?

Speaking at the 2008 annual conference of the British Pregnancy Advisory Service (BPAS), CEO Ann Furedi said:

> "We expect to be able to protect ourselves against pregnancy, we expect our birth control to work (though it doesn't always), and we expect to be able to right the wrong when it fails us."[28]

What we find is that (whether men and women actually acknowledge this or not) with the ready availability of abortion, for many this will quickly seem to be the easiest – if not the only – choice in an unplanned pregnancy. For some, this decision can be made within a few seconds of the pregnancy being discovered, even by those who never thought they would have an abortion. A woman in a crisis pregnancy has three options: she can give birth and parent the child; she can release the child for adoption, or she can have an abortion. For all practical purposes, a woman in this position – whose expectation of contraception has not been met – may think that abortion is the only realistic choice. Subconsciously, the thought "if I get pregnant I will have an abortion" may have been in her mind since she was a teenager, and this can be a powerful driver towards abortion. Now she is pregnant that thought seems increasingly reasonable.

Women may go through all the stages of welcoming the pregnancy, knowing in their heart of hearts that they will end it. I believe that this is due to the attitude of society, which pervades all of our thinking. It is almost as if society has hijacked our thought processes and we cannot think outside the box. We may not be able to imagine being able to deviate from the norm and actually bring up a child in circumstances that are far from ideal.

Writing in *The Times* in 2007, journalist and mother Caitlin Moran made this frank analysis of her own decision to have an abortion when she became unexpectedly pregnant:

> "Last year I had an abortion and I can honestly say it was one of the least difficult decisions of my life. I'm not being flippant when I say it took me longer to decide on what worktops to have in my kitchen than whether I was prepared to spend the rest of my life being responsible for a further human being."[29]

In practice, the option of placing a child for adoption is rarely chosen. Nicky-Sue once asked a pregnant woman whether she had considered adoption as an option instead of abortion, to which she replied, "If I am going to go through the pregnancy, I will keep the child." It seems that women can often contemplate abortion but not adoption. Another response can be, "I could never give the child away; only a bad mother would do that." For some people today, abortion can be seen as more compassionate than adoption.

For some women, the process of smothering unwelcome thoughts will be easy, for others it will be almost impossible. Many enjoy being pregnant, and do all the things they should for a healthy pregnancy: stop drinking and smoking and eat the right food. They may also allow themselves to bond with the child. They may work out the due date of the baby and toy with the idea of giving birth. They may go back and forth between deciding to keep the child and deciding to have an abortion, seeking advice from many people without really making up their minds. They may take folic acid and look at baby clothes in the shops, at the same time as making an appointment with an abortion clinic. The dilemma experienced through this is acute and very painful. Many feel thoroughly overwhelmed by what is happening to them. This is how the women on our course describe their experience of pregnancy leading up to the abortion. It can become a time of fear and confusion.

## The head versus the heart

For some women, it is as if a war literally breaks out inside them between their heads and their hearts. As the pregnancy progresses, the heart begins to call – the instinct to bond with and protect the child can rise up inside a woman and overwhelm her. "Save your child, give life to your baby," the heart pleads. A storm hits – a whirlwind of confusion and doubt driven by the mounting realisation that an abortion will end the life growing within her womb. This realisation can be really frightening. She suddenly feels overwhelmed, terrified, boxed in, deserted and alone.

In this crisis of head versus heart, the head has the power – it will make the decision. But the heart fights back with wave after wave of different emotions.

## Building a wall around her heart, developing tunnel vision

The women on our course often describe how, in order to make the decision for an abortion, they had to build a wall around their hearts, blocking off their maternal instinct and excitement about having the child. Only then could they bear to take the necessary steps to go through with the abortion.

As the day of the abortion approaches, the women and men we have spoken with have related how they developed tunnel vision, focusing on the abortion as the solution. They consciously block out unwelcome feelings and doubts so that abortion becomes the obvious choice. It appears to offer a way out, the ability to get off the 'roller coaster'.

Above all, it offers the tantalising possibility that within a few days or weeks, all this difficulty and stress will be forgotten, and life will return to where it was before the pregnancy was discovered. As people smother their doubts, the abortion clinic may be seen as a place of refuge from the storm and an island of peace that offers protection: a place of non-judgment, sympathy and understanding.

My heart has gone out to every woman and man I have met in a crisis pregnancy. At a time when their world has been turned upside down, someone is offering to wind back the clock, to put them back to where they were – just a simple procedure and the turmoil will stop and life will be back to normal. Talking to people in a crisis pregnancy, it can be tempting to agree that abortion might well be the best course of action in a seemingly hopeless situation. However, my experience on the post-abortion course has shown me that often people in a crisis pregnancy who chose abortion simply exchange one set of problems for another.

# Chapter 3

## What happens after an abortion?

### The key to understanding the sensitivities and introducing effective change

*[Although abortion can affect men, the first part of this chapter will focus on the experience of women. The experience of men is discussed later in the chapter.]*

It may seem counter-intuitive to think about abortion from the perspective of what happens afterwards, but I believe the experience of the women and men we have counselled over the years reveals something which comes as a surprise. That is, how deeply they bonded with the child in the womb before the abortion, and the effects that this can have afterwards. This goes a long way to explain the sensitivities, and I believe shows us the way to introduce effective change and break the silence with compassion and humility.

In the last chapter we saw how those choosing abortion tend to develop 'tunnel vision', and smother unwelcome thoughts and feelings. Their hope is that the turmoil they are experiencing will stop and be forgotten soon afterwards. However, for some, life after an abortion can turn out to be more complicated than they realised. At the heart of the issue lies the memory of the pregnancy. Women and men choose abortion because they do not wish the pregnancy to continue. But after a termination, the fact that they were once pregnant has the unexpected potential to maintain a powerful and unwelcome link to the past that cannot easily be broken or forgotten. For some, unwelcome thoughts and feelings can surface and begin to have a profound effect on their lives.

After an abortion, people seem to be divided into one of two groups. First, are those who are seemingly unaffected by their experience. And second, those who are, to a greater or lesser degree, affected by it. I believe that the degree to which an abortion will affect someone is based on a complex mix of personality, life experience, the circumstances surrounding the pregnancy and abortion, and the degree to which someone makes their life work afterwards.

For some, but not all, the after-effects seem to be influenced by pre-existing mental health problems or behavioural issues that perhaps contributed to the abortion decision in the first place. However, my personal view is that it would be a mistake to view emotional complications after an abortion as something that happens only to those who have a latent or pre-existing behavioural or mental health problem. It seems to me that sometimes the strongest, most confident and highly-educated people can be just as affected as those with a history of dysfunctional relationships or depression that pre-dated their abortion.

Indeed, it might be possible to argue the opposite for some. On the course, we noted that women and men for whom an abortion was their first setback in life, or their first serious encounter with an emotional trauma or problem, seemed particularly vulnerable to after-effects. It seemed that this group might lack the experience or coping strategies that others with pre-existing problems might have developed before their abortions, and which might have helped them cope afterwards. Other factors that seemed to leave individuals vulnerable to strong after-effects were situations where a high degree of pressure was applied by others (for example parents or partners), or the abortion went against strongly held personal religious, moral or cultural beliefs.

So, while it is fair to say that sometimes an abortion can sit on top of other behavioural or emotional problems – which perhaps contributed to the pregnancy and subsequent abortion – for many, the fact that we were able to help them deal with their problems within the context of our group would seem to point to the abortion as the direct cause. This is what those on our courses have told us.

For some, an abortion can act as an impetus to make their life work. Perhaps this group views it as a narrow escape and the abortion can be seen in positive terms, allowing their new, 'redeemed' life to happen; a new start as it were. For those who are able to move on and rebuild a successful life, perhaps including success at work or with a partner or family, the abortion may appear to recede into the past and be forgotten. However, even for this group, feelings or events may subsequently (sometimes suddenly) trigger a powerful connection with the abortion experience, often many years after the event.

In our groups, one woman felt overwhelmed when a subsequent, wanted child was born. Pictures of foetal development that she saw in a magazine shocked another woman. Another met up with a friend whose child had been born around the time of her abortion, and seeing the child suddenly connected her to her lost pregnancy.

Life changes, such as the onset of menopause, can also act as a trigger mechanism for a woman. Emotions arising from these events can be unexpectedly powerful when they do occur, because they have not been processed or resolved. The emotion can thus be experienced as if the abortion had only happened the day before.

It is our belief that anyone who experiences an abortion has the potential to make this subsequent connection. There is a saying that 'time heals'. From what we have seen in the men and women on our courses, time can be a part of the healing, but on its own it is not a healing process. The emotional effects of an abortion can surface powerfully many years after the event. We do not know why some do not make a subsequent connection; we run the course for those who do, so we have gained some insight as to why people do make this connection.

Our conclusions about the after-effects of abortion are based on discussions within our course, and I make no claim independently of this. Although I believe that the experience represented here may well be widespread, I know it is not universal and that many women and men go through abortion seemingly untouched. My purpose here is not to speculate as to the number of women and men who may have been impacted by abortion, but to explore its effects from the perspective of someone who *has* made a subsequent connection with their abortion experience. I believe that it is this perspective that can lead to a deeper understanding of the subject.

## What happens afterwards?

Immediately after an abortion many women feel enormous relief and immerse themselves in their lives again, trusting that everything will go back to normal. They cling to the belief that the abortion was just a medical procedure and was the best option for everyone concerned. They may heavily invest their energy in all the reasons why they could not have the child, such as their schoolwork, relationships with their partners, their social lives, their studies at university, their careers, or their families.

Others immediately feel that they have done something that is going to cause them pain. They experience an emptiness inside, and feel regret for the loss of their child. They may feel they have done something wrong, even something unforgivable. As a woman's hormones readjust, she may experience mood swings and unpleasant memories of the day the abortion took place.

In the face of this, women try to push the whole experience to the back of their minds. It is as if they take a big metal storage box and put everything to do with the abortion into it: their fears and agonies in making the decision, their memories of the abortion itself, their desires for a child and their thoughts about the child they have lost and what he or she might have been. Then they push the box into the darkest corner of their mind, put a large padlock on it, and carry on, pretending that the box is not there.

However, sooner or later they may find that this is not the end of the story. Something has changed: something physical, emotional or spiritual. It may be a feeling of sadness or a creeping guilt. They may begin to feel alone and distant from others: depressed, emotionless, worthless and perhaps angry with those who contributed to the abortion decision.

They may respond to these feelings by trying harder to make their lives work, but some women find over time that their efforts are in vain. Into that box they have put painful feelings and memories, or a determination not to acknowledge the child as a child. Equally, these women may have put good things in there: the desire to be a parent, their self-respect, their tenderness as a lover, so they are then cut off from these positive things. If we return to the image of the wall that a woman can build around her heart before the abortion, there can be so much of herself locked in behind the wall that her emotions, both good and bad, can become a jumble – impossible to deal with, but endlessly felt.

For these women, the sense of loss and self-blame may gradually increase as the pressure builds from within. They may stop liking themselves, believing they are bad people. They may seek to quench these negative feelings in a variety of ways: striving to be a success, or to be a perfect mother to their other children, keeping busy, perhaps using alcohol or living a promiscuous lifestyle. All in an attempt to hide from the thoughts and emotions leaking out of the big metal storage box they are trying to keep buried in the corner.

Some may feel they deserve punishment and either inflict it on themselves or allow themselves to receive it from others. If they have acknowledged the child as a child, they may not feel that they have the right to grieve their loss, which may cause a lingering, unresolved sorrow. There is often a feeling that something has been taken away by the abortion.

On our course we have seen people put a wide range of these and other issues behind them. These include: depression, eating disorders, sleep problems, feelings of unworthiness, self-punishment, low self-esteem, alcohol or drug misuse, and many other behaviours that appeared to be linked to a past abortion.

## Men and abortion

Although fewer men than women have attended our post-abortion courses, we have seen that men can be affected by abortion in exactly the same way. Everything written above about the dynamics of abortion and its effects is equally applicable to men. They can undergo the same feelings and encounter the same effects. Perhaps the point is most easily illustrated by the fact that we use *exactly* the same course for both men and women.

As with women, we believe not all men are affected by an abortion, but many are, and the effects of abortion on men are well known and attested.[30] We have helped men overcome the same types of problems including, on one occasion, an eating disorder connected to a past abortion.

There may be some nuanced differences, but basically men and women go through the same healing process during the course. With the realisation that he could have been a father, a man can come to see his behaviour as a cowardly act, abandoning his child and the woman to abortion. This can weigh heavily on him and he may come to see himself as having failed as a protector, as a provider or as a man. In turn, this might influence his self-confidence and his ability to commit to relationships.

## What causes the effects?

I believe that to create and nurture life is one of our deepest and most profound instincts as human beings. For many women, few experiences can compare to the wonder felt when they discover that they are pregnant, especially for the first time, even if they did not want to be. Pregnancy bestows a mantle of parenthood upon a woman, and also upon a man.

At the moment a woman discovers she is pregnant she becomes a mother. A man becomes a father. A life has begun. When a woman becomes pregnant both her body, and her mind, start to prepare for the arrival of her child. Her maternal instincts may begin to come into play, even if she is planning to end the pregnancy with an abortion. The truth is that without an abortion a child would have been born. Five or six months later a birth would have taken place.

**The fact is that abortion is not a time machine; it does not turn back the clock, or take a woman back to where she was before she became pregnant. It does not make a woman as if she had never been pregnant. She will always be a woman who has experienced a pregnancy.**

At a very deep level, pregnancy – no matter how brief – connects men and women with their child. Abortion leaves them suspended or disconnected. People may not like to think that a child is growing in the womb before an abortion, but afterwards the memory of the pregnancy, and of the bond that was established at the discovery of the pregnancy, can maintain a powerful connection with the lost child.

Some will have a clear sense of whether their child was a boy or a girl. Some, out of an unconscious longing, may have named their child. They may have an idea of the colour of his or her eyes, of their hair. They may experience intense dreams of the child in their sleep. Some will know exactly to the day when that child would have been born and every year they will remember the due date, and be aware of the exact age the child would have been. For some, the images of the child grow in their minds as the years pass, so they can see how they would have looked as they grew older. One man said this:

"I was with a group of friends and we started talking about abortion. I mentioned that a girlfriend of mine had once had an abortion and someone asked, "If the child had been born, how old would they be today?" Without thinking I answered "Twelve and a half years old". The hairs on the back of my neck went up. How had I known that? If you had asked me when my girlfriend had the abortion I would not have known, not to within two or three years. I thought I had forgotten all about it, yet here I was all those years later knowing exactly how old the child would have been."

This conversation was the start of a journey of healing for that man, who later undertook a post-abortion recovery course.

On our course, opportunity is given for women and men to express their feeling through letters, poems or artwork. The work they create can be intense in its longing and sensuality: they portray vivid images of the lost children; their longing to hold and nurture them; to see them grow; to take their first steps, to gaze into their eyes. Their yearning is powerful, and real.

Some reading this who may not have thought about the effects of abortion before may think that a course such as ours is mawkish, or might encourage harmful self-indulgence and that people should simply 'get over it'. But let us consider the loss of miscarriage. Those who have experienced this will know that it can be felt as a searing pain, and every bit as keenly as the loss of a baby carried to full-term. It can be felt years after the event as the lost child is still mourned and remembered.

The connection with the child experienced after an abortion has the potential to be as powerful as with a miscarried child or even a born child. Those who do make this connection can find themselves in a place of grief and darkness, and we have seen on our courses the depths of grief expressed as women wept for their lost children. I have also witnessed men weeping as they made a similar connection. We do not tell them what to think and we do not push them into feeling or thinking anything. We let them make their own connections, in their own time, at whatever level is useful to them. But for both men and women there can be an almost overwhelming sense of loss and sorrow.

But they are then also confronted with another terrible reality: the part they personally played in deciding to end the pregnancy. For some, the growing realisation that they have participated in denying their child the opportunity of life can leave them in a place of pain, feeling that they have done something terrible, something unforgivable.

## The key sensitivity

Most women and men on our courses discover that they have been living with the sub-conscious thought, 'I participated in ending the life of my child' buried deep in their hearts. This has been the hardest area to write about for this book, and it has taken us many years to speak these words out in public and to put them in writing. For twenty years Nicky-Sue and I avoided saying this, and on the course itself found it extremely difficult to deal with the issues raised by this terrible truth. Try as we might to avoid any direct mention of it, the women themselves nearly always made this connection, and for them resolving this issue was what brought release and healing.

## Why is all this important?

One third of our entire population is potentially carrying around, to a lesser or greater extent, buried and unacknowledged feelings of grief and guilt connected with a past abortion. At the beginning of the post-abortion course, the first emotion to surface is usually one of anger, which is deep-seated and sometimes bordering on rage. The anger can be directed towards others, for example a partner, parents, or the system of abortion itself, but often it is functioning as a self-protection mechanism. People can build a wall of anger (or sometimes other emotions) either to shield themselves from the nihilistic and overwhelming thought that they have participated in ending the life of their own child, or to protect themselves from their feelings of loss or grief. Others can sense this anger associated with the subject, so no wonder abortion can be such a touchy subject both inside and outside the church!

Therefore, understanding what happens after an abortion is important for three reasons:

First, while it may at first appear counter-intuitive to think about abortion from the perspective of those who have been through it, by now I am hoping that you have glimpsed what life can be like for some of those who have experienced abortion, and begin to see some of the obvious sensitivities. Given the scale of what is going on it is not surprising that the subject of abortion can become a sensitive 'no-go' area in church communities, and leaders can feel they have had their heads bitten off if they raise the subject.

Second, by understanding the sensitivities, we can also see the importance of bringing healing to those who are hurting. While it may appear compassionate to avoid the subject of abortion, the resulting silence is not of use to those who are hurting, but neither is judgment or condemnation. What is needed is an engaged, knowledgeable and balanced approach to the subject with compassion and God's love at its heart.

Third, understanding what happens after an abortion can help us make a connection with the subject in a way that traditional thinking does not. Sometimes when I talk with groups about abortion someone will say something like, "Well, that all depends on when you think life begins." This question seems to frame much thinking about abortion. I believe that it is completely the wrong question. A much better question to ask is, "What does the experience of men and women who maintain a connection with their abortion afterwards tell us about when life begins?" To this there can only be one answer: for them the life began before they discovered that they were pregnant, perhaps at conception itself. This is what their experience tells them about when a human life begins.

A contemporary audience can struggle to connect with the fact that a life begins at conception if they think in terms of the question, "Has a life begun?" In an unplanned pregnancy, concern for a woman can override what can be seen as an academic point regarding when life begins. But through the experience of women and men who retain a strong connection with a past abortion, we begin to see at a meaningful level that an abortion is a process that ends a life, and for those who have maintained a connection, that child will at one level or another be missed for the rest of their lives. Abortion does not seem such a simple act when this is understood. This is the terrible truth about abortion, and one that can open the door to understanding and healing.

# Chapter 4

## Introducing effective change in the church

### Navigating the sensitivities by learning the lessons of the last forty years

> *The definition of madness is to keep doing the same thing and expect a different result! (Traditional proverb)*

Reviewing the Christian response to abortion over the last forty years, there are some simple lessons to be learnt, which I believe could help transform the way that abortion is perceived and talked about within the church. Furthermore, I believe that by effecting a few simple changes in the church and playing to traditional Christian strengths of love and pastoral care, Christians could then begin to have an impact on our wider culture.

### The need for a different approach, beginning with the church

If nothing is said or done, the abortion rate will continue at the current alarmingly high rate, and could possibly increase. What is needed is the forging of a new worldview that could lead a new generation away from abortion. If such a worldview cannot be created within the church, then it is unlikely it would succeed outside. The church is a logical place to start, since church communities are accustomed to gathering together and hearing difficult issues discussed, and the basis of faith unites Christians behind shared values, and the work of the Holy Spirit convicts of the truth.

However, traditional church teaching on abortion does not engage a contemporary Christian audience, many of whom have been brought up to view abortion as a regrettable but compassionate response to a an unplanned pregnancy. A new apologetic is needed, one in which assumptions about an audience's beliefs should not be made. Since many Christians are ambivalent about abortion, for perfectly understandable reasons, it is helpful to be prepared to explore people's doubts and questions. In addressing this subject, not only through teaching sermons, but also in other areas of church life and in our own hearts and minds, we can help to end the silence that has grown up around this subject, a silence which we have seen is not compassionate, but destructive.

The stories of women (and sometimes men) who have made a powerful connection with a past abortion – such as those we have counselled over the years – can add the missing dimension to our thinking and help those who might not otherwise think about abortion make a deep connection with the subject. However, this is not about getting post-abortive women and their partners to testify against abortion in public as part of a campaign. Rather, it is about understanding their experience and letting this mould a more realistic worldview about when a life begins in the womb.

## The need for compassionate language and presentation

I once attended a packed Christian event at the Albert Hall in London to pray for revival. The first speaker was a Member of Parliament who spoke resoundingly about abortion. As he finished his speech he punched the air and shouted, "…and I believe that abortion is MURDER!" before sitting down to thunderous applause.

My heart froze. It just so happened that we had started one of our post-abortion recovery courses three weeks before, with six women who were now at a very sensitive stage. I knew that many of them were planning to attend this revival event and so when the cry "Abortion is murder!" went out, I immediately thought of each of them. The following week they told me that they had been very upset by the remark. One said she felt as if the whole of the Albert Hall had turned around and pointed at her, shouting, "There she is – the murderess who murdered her child."

Admittedly, this event was some time ago, but it serves as a good example of the sensitivities and the need for Christians to reflect the grace of God in all that we say and do when it comes to abortion. Language and presentation need to be thought through and the issues and sensitivities understood.

Often there is a tendency among those addressing the subject of abortion to use unhelpful language and symbols. This is a sensitive subject, and it is important to bear in mind that there will be people in every audience who may have been directly affected by abortion themselves. Therefore, we should be prepared to minister to them by being humble and compassionate in thought and speech.

Insensitive vocabulary, such as, "murder", "kill", "evil", "blood of the innocents", and so on, is counterproductive and should never be used. Pictures of aborted foetuses, designed to shock, can cause offence and are hurtful to those who have been through abortion. We seek to make abortion unthinkable, but the use of these words and symbols can achieve the opposite effect by making speakers seem bigoted and judgmental and by driving Christians away from traditional church doctrine. When it comes to forgiveness, we must become the reckless dispensers of God's grace, not his miserly doorkeepers offering forgiveness on our own terms.

## The need to establish a 'just culture' in the church

In the aviation industry the Civil Aviation Authority (CAA) have introduced a new concept of promoting a 'just culture' within aviation organisations as part of a safety initiative to reduce accidents. The idea is that by introducing an open and honest reporting culture, pilots and engineers are free to admit mistakes without sanction. This counters a natural human tendency to be secretive and cover up mistakes. In a 'just culture' mistakes are not only admitted, but also published and advertised so that others can learn from them.

The CAA defines a 'just culture' as one in which "individuals are not punished for actions, omissions or decisions taken by them which result in a reportable event". It adds, however, "Gross negligence, willful violations and destructive acts are not tolerated."[31]

I believe that there are lessons to be learned from this approach in creating a 'just culture' in the church when it comes to abortion. There is a natural tension between the church's desire to protect family values and its desire to avoid situations that fall short of the ideal. Unmarried Christian men and women in a crisis pregnancy are acutely sensitive to the possibility of public shame and condemnation within their churches, and this can become a contributing factor to an abortion decision. On a recent course, one woman shared the fact that she was too afraid to admit to the pregnancy in the church, knowing the church's teaching on sex before marriage, so instead she had an abortion. Another was asked to leave her church by senior leaders when the pregnancy became known, and she subsequently felt that this rejection contributed significantly to her decision for an abortion.

Therefore, to establish a 'just culture' in our churches we need to make room for people to admit mistakes without fear of shame or sanction.

Most Christian leaders are only too aware of the inevitability of error and unwise choices within the church community. The challenge before them is how to maintain the balance between this reality of life and the desire to teach God's standards for living, so that abortion is not chosen simply to avoid condemnation. Replacing a perceived culture of judgment and condemnation with one that clearly accepts and supports anyone who experiences an unintended pregnancy, may help to overcome the barriers of shame that might contribute to a decision for abortion. To do this may require thinking differently, but it is imperative to ensure that our church culture and structures do not inadvertently push people into abortion.

In discussing this with church leaders I have been asked if encouraging women to keep their children means that the church has to provide materially for them. While any material assistance that the church can provide to individuals would be welcomed, actually I have seen from my experience counselling couples with an unplanned pregnancy that so often it is affirmation and encouragement to think differently that can make the difference. Our culture is so heavily weighted towards abortion that sometimes simply speaking positively about giving birth, and making it clear that this is accepted gives a woman the courage and impetus to make a different decision.

If abortion is to become less likely in our midst, we need to be welcoming and understanding of people as they struggle to come to terms with the circumstances that, while far from ideal, have not ended in abortion. We need to be accepting and supportive of the unconventional. Every parent feels they are not good enough, and people facing an unplanned pregnancy who courageously choose to give birth do not need anyone to add to their troubles. What they need is encouragement, respect and friends to cheer them on as they swim against the tide of abortion in our culture.

It is helpful to ask what the church leadership's response would be to a man or woman in a position of leadership who found themselves with an unplanned pregnancy outside of marriage. This would need careful consideration and handling. On our post-abortion courses we have heard stories from both men and women (including those in leadership), who have been publicly humiliated and expelled from their churches when either an unintended pregnancy or an abortion came to light. This action is unhelpful and damaging as it lacks compassion and promotes a culture of secrecy around abortion, thus having the potential to make future abortions more, rather than less, likely. Individual circumstances and behaviour can be very complicated, and each case has to be taken on its own merits, but from my personal observation as a man running our ministry, I have noticed that if there is a fall-out after an abortion the woman seems to receive more blame than the man.

Practically speaking, it would be helpful if individual church communities could discuss and be prepared for the action they would take in the event of an unintended pregnancy. Does the congregation understand the church leadership's position of unconditional acceptance? If not, would it be helpful to consider a public statement from the senior leader to this effect? Christians experiencing an unintended pregnancy may find it difficult to come to church fearing gossip and condemnation. Are there any steps that could be taken to encourage them to keep coming to church?

## The need for education and information

Many people have very little knowledge or understanding of the issues surrounding abortion, or of the powerful currents that flow unseen in our society. A basic knowledge of the dynamics that lead to abortion could help us to avoid it in our own lives, and to enter into a wider dialogue with friends, family and the wider culture, thus hopefully breaking the silence effectively and with compassion and understanding. In addition, teaching is needed for the many Christians today who have little knowledge of how the church has historically responded to abortion, or how to apply biblical teaching to the subject.

## Focusing on a personal response

The main danger for Christians lies in having an academic or compartmentalised understanding of abortion that does not enable an individual to follow his or her beliefs through when faced with a crisis. In the only survey of its kind ever undertaken among a group of women who had terminated their pregnancies, 75% thought that abortion was morally wrong up to the point when they became pregnant. This belief did not deter them from proceeding with their abortions[32], which shows that it is not enough to believe that abortion is morally wrong, or that we would not have an abortion ourselves. The key is to encourage individuals to engage with the issue at a meaningful level, and to respond personally by understanding the risks and taking action to avoid them. The following chapter will outline the key issues that would be helpful for individual Christians to be aware of and think through.

## Introducing change from the bottom up, rather than imposing it from the top down

Over the years, it has been seen that seeking to impose a minority view on the majority through the legal or legislative process has not brought about change. To transform our society's thinking on abortion I would suggest that thinking needs to be changed from the bottom up, rather than by running a campaign. Everyone, including abortion providers, would agree that reducing unintended pregnancy rates is desirable, and that in an ideal world there would be no need for abortion.[33]

In his book *Making Abortion Rare*, David Reardon suggests that instead of trying to make abortion illegal, Christians should focus on making it, "Unthinkable for pregnant women. Unthinkable for loved ones to whom they will turn when faced with a crisis pregnancy."[34]

Making abortion illegal could simply create a vast market in backstreet abortion and abortion tourism, where people travel to countries where it is legal. In any event, with the advent of RU 486 (the abortion pill), it is now possible to supply a medical abortion anywhere in the world by post, thus fairly easily making illegal abortion widely available. So in many ways the legal status of abortion is just a technicality.

Making abortion unthinkable is a much more practical aim, requiring a broader approach: the transformation of our culture by influencing values, thus removing the demand for abortion. This is also a more achievable way of working because it is possible to start on a small scale by working with individuals, small groups and local church communities.

## Finding the right language to communicate with those of no faith

We should be able to communicate Christian doubts about abortion to those outside the Christian faith, in a way that can be understood and accepted. Whilst reflecting the biblical value that life is to be highly respected, what we say should not be tied exclusively to the Bible or belief in God.

In some contexts it may not be helpful to say, "God says…" or, "The Bible says…." Instead we can learn to help those without a Christian faith to find the eternal values that give us a shared sense of right and wrong. Ecclesiastes 3:11 says, "He has also set eternity in the human heart." God has set a sense of right and wrong in all of us, and our challenge is to find ways to convey the truth that abortion is destructive. In this context, the stories of women and men who have been through abortion have the power to win hearts and change minds.

Christians know how to respond to the hurts and difficulties caused by abortion by bringing the gift of healing to our local communities. Through the ministry of pastoral care and post-abortion recovery we are able to meet a genuine need and develop a consensus around shared values with those outside of our faith.

## Moulding an effective response

There are four key areas in which we can allow the above lessons to shape our response as Christians:

### 1. In our personal response

The first place where we should try to make abortion unthinkable is in our own lives. This requires a personal response and a willingness to change. Individuals should be encouraged to allow the facts of abortion and an understanding of post-abortion dynamics to inform their views, and to take action to ensure that they do not inadvertently expose themselves to the risk of an abortion in their own lives. Perhaps the definitive Christian response that we seek to mould is quite simply this: "To resolve not to have an abortion in our own lives and to live this out as an intentional value."

### 2. In our families

Within our own families, it would be most helpful to create an environment where parents could discuss with each other the dynamics that lead to abortion, and then continue this dialogue with their teenage children. The booklet, *Unplanned Pregnancy: Talking with Teenagers* has been designed to facilitate such a discussion within families.

### 3. In our own church communities

Within our church communities, simple actions can be taken to promote a compassionate discussion of abortion, and to create a 'just culture' that leads away from it. We need not only to unite behind the idea that abortion is wrong, but also to believe the right thing for the right reason.

## 4. In our social outreach and mission

Perhaps the greatest opportunity for the church lies in the area of pastoral care and post-abortion recovery, where we can bring the desperately needed message of God's love and forgiveness to those who are hurting. This will enable the church to influence our local communities and culture, through practical expressions of unconditional love that demonstrate the love of the Saviour to a fallen world.

# Chapter 5

## Shaping an effective personal view

> *"Teacher, which is the greatest commandment in the Law?" Jesus replied: "'Love the Lord your God with all your heart and with all your soul and with all your mind.' This is the first and greatest commandment. And the second is like it: 'Love your neighbour as yourself'" (Mathew 22:34–40).*

When it comes to abortion what does it mean to love the Lord your God "with all your heart and with all your soul and with all your mind"?

One would have to have a heart of stone not to see how abortion can appear to be the most obvious solution to a crisis pregnancy. It seems so simple, so easy: just a little procedure and the situation will go away. My heart has gone out to every woman I have met in a crisis pregnancy, and to every man whose partner is facing an abortion. It can be easy to see each individual as an exception and to believe that, just in this case, an abortion would be the right decision. It can be a struggle at times to see the issue clearly.

John Wimber, the American founder of Vineyard Ministries, once said, "I am just a fat man trying to get to heaven." By this I think he meant that we are all sinners living in a fallen world, trying to do the right thing, to make sense of the world through our faith as best we can, to serve the Lord with all our hearts, with all our souls and with all our minds. I believe that in the area of abortion, allowing our faith to transform us through the renewing of our minds does not mean being judgmental or narrow-minded, but allowing our faith to shape our response to a crisis, and to take actions consistent with our faith. Ultimately, we may need to set aside a convenient solution and be prepared to wrestle with difficulties, but even if we get it wrong we know that we can trust in the grace, mercy and love of Jesus Christ.

Some may think they have a clear-cut view of the subject, and that they themselves would never have an abortion. But life can turn out to be more complicated than we think. One woman joined our course having had an abortion a few years previously. She was bright and intelligent with an excellent career. She had been raised in a Christian family and would say she had a strong Christian faith all her life.

She had one real passion from her early teenage years, and that passion was campaigning against abortion. She was horrified by it, knew a lot about it and campaigned against it vigorously. She even picketed abortion clinics, handing out leaflets to people going in for abortions. Yet when she found herself unexpectedly pregnant, *she had an abortion.*

In 2000, a paper entitled *The Only Moral Abortion is My Abortion* was published online.[35] An abortion clinic employee who noticed that someone who had previously been protesting outside her clinic had come in to have an abortion undertook this international study.

She mentioned this to some of her colleagues who told her similar stories from their own experience. She then corresponded with other abortion clinics around the world and collated some of the many stories of this phenomenon.

The case studies make fascinating reading. One example tells of a mother and daughter who had both been protesting outside an abortion clinic one day. Then the mother brought her daughter in for an abortion the following day, and both were back on the protest line the next! One woman interviewed justified her action by saying, "The only moral abortion is my abortion", prompting the title of the paper. I don't know the author personally, and I have no way of checking her sources, but from our experience, the stories ring true.

So, clearly there seems to be a gap between the way people think about abortion and what they may actually do when crunch time comes. Having read the above story, we may think that this would never happen to us, but as the story warns, even those who thought they had a clear-cut view may end up having an abortion.

What, then, should be the correct Christian response to this issue? I would suggest that it is this: *that Christians should resolve not to have an abortion and to live this out as an intentional value in their own lives.* I believe this is what it would mean to "Love the Lord your God with all your heart and with all your soul and with all your mind" in relation to this issue.

However, given the prevalence of abortion in the culture around us, I believe that avoiding abortion requires a high degree of intentionality. It requires an awareness of the dangers, and actively taking action to avoid them. Taking the following deliberate steps would help achieve this aim.

## 1. Understanding that abortion is a personal issue, and that as individuals we are at risk

We may all have a stereotype in our minds of the sort of person we imagine might have an abortion. It might be a teenager or someone pregnant from a one-night stand, or perhaps someone who has had the terrible misfortune of being raped. Whatever our thoughts are about the sort of person who might have an abortion, the one person we might think it will not be is someone like *me*. We assume abortion only happens to people who are not like us, but statistically, it is something that happens more or less across all sections of our society. Statistically, people who have abortions are people just like you and me.

Therefore, we need to think the issue through for ourselves, and think through beforehand what would be our response to an unexpected crisis, either in our own lives or the lives of our friends or family. Nobody deliberately sets out to have an abortion, but it seems to me that the first step on the road to an abortion clinic is not having thought through a personal response to a crisis. Unless we, as individuals, have a consistent view that will shape our behaviour and actions, we may be tempted by the wrong set of circumstances to be influenced by the decisions that many around us are making. We also need to understand the highly institutionalised nature of abortion in our society, and that most medical professionals will assume that an abortion will be desired in the case of an unintended pregnancy.

The view that we form about abortion should be expressed in a compassionate and sensitive way, with an awareness that, due to the fact that one third of women and men will have experienced abortion in our culture, in any setting there could be men and women for whom abortion is a difficult personal issue. We need to let God's grace abound in everything we say and do, and ensure that love and compassion forms the basis of our response. We must ensure that what we say does not become a stumbling block for the work of the gospel. This does not mean staying silent, but it does mean avoiding insensitive language.

## 2. Understanding our ability to control our fertility, even if contraception is used, is limited

Every year in Britain, around 850,000 conceptions take place. Around 200,000 of these will be terminated by an abortion.[36]

The truly astonishing fact about these conceptions is not just the abortion rate. Rather, even though at any one time 75% of the population aged 18–44 uses contraception,[37] around 50% of conceptions are unintended pregnancies.

**Half of ALL pregnancies in the United Kingdom are unintended.**[38]

This situation in not only found in the United Kingdom, it is also seen across the developed world. Professor James Trussell, director of population research at Princeton University and expert in population trends and contraception, comments on the situation in America:

> "What is, to me, the most mind-boggling statistic is that half (48%) of women aged 15–44 in the US have had an unintended pregnancy. So when you walk down a street in New York, half of the women will have had an unintended pregnancy."[39]

Therefore we need to let our personal expectation of our ability to control our fertility, even if contraception is used, be shaped by the fact that in practice we cannot always prevent conception, and to allow this fact to influence our decisions about sexual relationships both before and after marriage. Christian men, in particular, should be challenged by this fact to take responsibility for their actions. (To re-iterate the point made in Chapter 2: contraception can be highly effective if used correctly, but in practice it is not always used correctly, leading to the high rate of unintended pregnancy.)

When making their choices, some Christians may also not be aware that some forms of contraception may act as a form of early abortion.

## 3. Having open discussions with our partners

None of us knows what pressures we will come under in life and Christians who choose abortion may do so because they are unprepared for what life suddenly throws at them. At the beginning of a relationship, people often discuss how they would like to control their fertility, but rarely discuss abortion and what they would do if an unintended pregnancy were experienced. I would suggest that time should be spent by couples exploring their values and what they might do, if faced with an unplanned pregnancy or tests for foetal abnormality, *before* they are in a potentially difficult situation. This may prevent much heartache in the future.

## 4. Being informed about adoption

Our culture has an overwhelmingly negative view of adoption. Therefore, it is helpful to allow a positive view of adoption as an empowering alternative to abortion inform our mindset. To counter negative stereotypes of adoption, it might help to understand how the modern adoption process works.

Adoption procedures are now quite different from what they used to be. Choosing adoption and what a mother wants for her baby can be considered at any time during pregnancy and after the child is born. It is fully accepted by adoption agencies that following the birth of a baby a mother needs time to recover and for her hormones to settle down again. Any decisions made within the first six weeks of birth will not be binding or acted upon. Every opportunity is given to the mother to reflect and review her decision and to be sure of her thoughts, her wishes and her feelings. Support and counselling are offered throughout to assist with this journey. In the early stages a mother may change her mind at any time, but as the adoption process develops and evolves it may take longer to be able to withdraw, especially once the child has been placed and has begun the essential bonding process with a new family.

A mother's wishes and preferences concerning how they want their child adopted will be actively considered, along with what is in the best interests for the child. If a woman decides upon adoption she is able to provide information about herself, the child's birth, early life and why the child was placed for adoption, if she would like to. This information is incorporated into a "Life Story Book" and can be given to the child in an age appropriate format by the adoption agency when the time is right. It can also be requested when a young adopted person reaches adulthood.

The Adoption and Children Act of 2002 now places a responsibility on the adoption agency to actively explore the views of the wider birth family, including the birth father and his family (if that is desired) about the new baby, and whether they wish to consider adopting the child. Their views are sought alongside considering an adoptive family. It is important to note however that the birth mother is not legally obliged to name the father of the baby on the birth certificate.

Adoption can be a very positive option and though it can be painful for the mother to relinquish the baby, and difficult at this stage to see the positives, there can be good outcomes for everyone involved. Some additional information on practical issues connected with adoption, together with the contact details for the charity ASIST are given at the end of this book.

## 5. Extreme Circumstances

When thinking about the issue of abortion, it may be helpful not to let extreme circumstances dominate our thinking. Many feel that in some exceptional situations, such as pregnancy following rape, abortion is an understandable and justifiable action. In Appendix I, I have given my response to this question, based on the experience of talking with women from our groups who have been in this tragic situation. They had some unusual thoughts on the subject that deserve to be listened to. Having thought about the issue, and listened to their stories, it is my personal belief that abortion is only helpful in situations to save a mother's life.

If a woman accepts that abortion is permissible in extreme circumstances, and then finds herself in a crisis pregnancy, this may well constitute 'extreme circumstances' to her, even though it is not as a result of an extreme circumstance such as rape. This is the mechanism by which people who are against abortion can end up choosing it, effectively saying, "The only moral abortion is my abortion". It is the tear in the fabric of their beliefs through which they can all too easily fall.

## 6. Resolving a past abortion

Those who have been through abortion can bring a wealth of experience and understanding to the issue. Therefore it would be really helpful for Christians who have had an abortion in the past to work through the consequences of this, coming to the point where they can think clearly about the past, lay it before God, and find peace in their hearts over the issue. Abortion is not the 'unforgiveable sin' and I would encourage Christians who may feel that they have unresolved difficulties to seek help in talking these through.

While some may be able to resolve the matter simply between themselves and God, if others wished to take it further or deeper, then post-abortion support is available through organisations such as CareConfidential in many parts of the country, and their post-abortion recovery programme is available through centres and online. Abortion can be very corrosive to faith, and our experience is that Christians who go through a structured healing process can find a new faith and walk with God. This is not about public confession or testimony: it is about finding peace in our own hearts and overcoming the unhelpful sensitivities that currently inhibit the open discussion of abortion within the church.

## Conclusion

Loving the Lord our God with all our hearts, minds and souls does not mean keeping silent on the issue of abortion. Loving our neighbour as ourselves does not mean being judgmental or bigoted, or entering into unhelpful actions or using unhelpful language. What is needed is a balanced, compassionate view that reflects the character and life of our Saviour in his mission to love a fallen and sinful world, and taking actions commensurate with that mission. In the final chapter I will suggest a few simple ways that I believe our society might be served in a way that could achieve this.

# Chapter 6

## How to win friends and influence people when speaking about abortion in a church setting

While as part of creating a 'just culture' a sermon might be preached, if leaders felt that the subject was too sensitive or inappropriate for a teaching programme, then simply holding a meeting among church leaders would make a start. (See Chapter 8 'Where to Start'.) A sermon could follow later when confidence has been gained.

Before considering how best to speak about the Christian view of abortion, it may be helpful to review the way this subject has been traditionally presented within the church context, under the heading, 'The Sanctity of Life'. Typically this type of presentation would be structured thus:

### 1. What does church history tell us about abortion?

*That throughout history the church has taught it is wrong, at least outside the context of saving a mother's life.*

## 2. What does the Bible say about abortion?

*Although the Bible makes no specific mention of abortion, most theologians are united in their view that the Bible condemns abortion.*

## 3. What does medical science tell us about abortion?

*That even foetuses as young as six weeks are fully human and highly developed. Only two logical choices remain – either life begins at conception or it does not.*

## 4. What do we think about so-termed 'hard cases' of abortion for reasons of rape, incest, or a medical disability?

*In these cases the child is still human and life should be preserved.*

## 5. The conclusion

*A foetus is fully human and has an independent right to life. Abortion is therefore the equivalent to an act of murder and should be made illegal.*

As a way of communicating the Christian view on abortion in our current culture, I suggest that this line of reasoning is not necessarily helpful. Indeed, its effect can be exactly the opposite of that intended by a speaker. For example, if the conclusion of the argument is that abortion ends the life of a child growing in the womb and should thus be made illegal, those who feel that abortion should be an available option for women will see this position as being judgmental or bigoted, whilst campaigners for abortion rights on the other hand, may be seen as the compassionate champions of women's health by their perceived success at preventing backstreet abortions. The Biblical or Christian view is thus dismissed out of hand.

The 'Sanctity of Life' reasoning also gives supremacy to the rights of the foetus over the woman, an approach that clashes with contemporary thinking, even amongst some in a Christian audience. By focusing on medical images and terms, the argument can seem remote, theoretical and academic, making abortion appear as the lesser of two evils to those facing the reality of a crisis pregnancy. Arguments surrounding rape, incest and medical disability can appear legalistic and alienate those in an audience who might otherwise think abortion is wrong. They also encourage people to think in extreme terms, which may not be helpful to the audience in developing a personal view.

Many church leaders would say that their aim in speaking about abortion in a church setting is to make it a less likely choice. I would argue that, paradoxically, the opposite effect may have been achieved: that the way abortion has been discussed within churches in recent times has actually made it more likely by driving it underground, and reinforcing the silence. Therefore, we need to meet people where they are at and not erect barriers that prevent communication. What we say needs to be sensitive and compassionate, not rooted in extreme or fearful thinking.

I am not saying that the sanctity of life should not be mentioned – far from it – one of the objectives of a talk should be to clearly re-affirm traditional biblical and church teaching on the subject. But this should be done briefly, with compassion, and should not form the main thrust of a talk or sermon. If people want to investigate the theology or history they can do so from a recommended reading list. It is more useful to address head on the more likely situations that people might encounter in their daily lives, either in their own families or in the culture around them.

If we do mention the subject of abortion, other than in a dedicated talk, we need to be prepared to engage with it at a deeper level, with an awareness that hurt can be caused by insensitivity. While there can be a temptation to mention the subject in passing, thus feeling that the issue has been addressed, this has the potential to cause great harm and achieves little.

Again, I am not suggesting that abortion should be avoided as a subject altogether, but careful thought and preparation are essential. One thoughtful approach that has its focus on both the woman and the child has been advocated by David Reardon of the Elliott Institute. He suggests that the word abortion should never be used unless it is sandwiched between engaging, broadly pro-woman statements. Traditionally, the debate has ignored the woman involved in an abortion and focused solely on the right of the foetus to life. The 'pro-woman sandwich' effectively shifts the focus of what is being said to include concerns for the mother.

David Reardon writes:

> "Dr Jack Willke [a renowned pro-life speaker] reports that over the years he and his wife Barbara have faced increasing levels of hostility during their foetal development presentations on college campuses. Their pro-life message was simply not penetrating the walls of defensive anger that they faced. But in the last two years they have begun preceding their talks with a five-minute introduction expressing their concern, understanding and compassion for women who have been through abortion, many of who felt that they had no other choice. Following the foetal information, they conclude with additional information about post-abortion syndrome and post-abortion recovery.
>
> "In essence, the Willkes have sandwiched foetal development between two layers of pro-woman compassion. According to

Dr Willke: 'The result has been almost dramatic… the anger and combativeness are gone. The questions are civil. We are listened to once again… Now they must take a new and serious look at this issue.'"[40]

## Laying the groundwork

If a talk on abortion is being planned, it might be helpful beforehand to form a consensus within the wider church leadership about what should be included.

As a first step, a meeting could be held to discuss the issue with the church's leadership team, and might include senior leaders, home group leaders, those with pastoral responsibility and any staff members. I would suggest it would be best to include as many people as possible. The idea is to forge a consensus over the values that you would like to promote in the area of abortion before talking about it openly in a church meeting. In particular the values that would underpin the creation of a 'just culture' would be key. (For example, how would you respond as a community to a woman with an unplanned pregnancy, or who once had an abortion, or to a man whose partner was in this position?) Agreeing an agenda and raising awareness of the need for compassionate language and presentation are important as a few wrong words (such one leader saying 'I believe abortion is murder'), could undo much of what could be achieved.

A training element is also important in order to equip leaders to meet and discuss the issue with someone coming forward for counselling or prayer about the issue (as discussed in Chapter 7). It would also be helpful to look at any other areas of church life that might benefit from discussion of issues surrounding abortion, such as youth and women's groups.

Before breaking the silence around abortion, it would also be helpful to have a prayer counselling referral system in place before any talk is delivered, or at least to think through and agree what response would be made to someone who, after a talk, wanted to discuss it as a personal issue. A referral system could be one or more nominated individuals, with all leaders understanding the necessity to provide the assurance of confidentiality. It is essential that pastoral oversight should be in place and that anyone volunteering to be part of a counselling referral system should be supervised and understand the need for disclosure to their supervisor of any safety or legal concerns with those being counselled. The following chapter will give advice on how to pray through the issue with a Christian.

It would be helpful to prepare additional material including a recommended reading list and contact details for further counselling arrangements (including outside organisations such as CareConfidential) to give out after the talk. Ideally, everyone would take away a leaflet or the relevant information as they leave so that those wanting help will not feel 'singled out' by, for example, having to walk to a table to pick up a leaflet. Email referral is an excellent way to build confidence in confidentiality. Try not to say, "Anyone who would like to pray about a past abortion should come and see me afterwards!"

## Suggested talk structure – the concept of 'defence in depth'

It can be difficult to know where to begin in planning a talk on abortion. Below are three headings that I suggest could form a useful structure for any talk on this subject.

In his book *Understanding Human Error*, Professor James Reason suggests the concept of "defence in depth" (sometimes known as the "Swiss Cheese Model"). His work has been widely used within industries such as aviation and oil exploration to develop a culture of safety, especially in situations where human error might result in a fatal accident. The idea behind defending in depth is an acknowledgement that human beings are subject to error (or as the philosopher Cicero suggested, "To err is human"). Therefore, it is not sufficient to have a set of rules or expectations of behaviour in order to avoid accidents. Working with the grain of human nature involves acknowledging the risk of error and building multiple layers to help protect against it. To achieve this Reason suggests using a mix of skill-based, rule-based and knowledge-based behaviour (as opposed to just rule-based behaviour) to provide the necessary depth of defence.

Christians today may have very little knowledge about abortion, little skill in thinking through the issue for themselves and talking about it with others, and a very vague understanding of the biblical perspective (what Christian theologians and historians have to say on the subject). As a basic structure, therefore, I would like to suggest that a talk on abortion could be divided into three sections under the following headings:

1. **Knowledge** – who has an abortion, why do they get pregnant, what happens to them afterwards?

2. **Framework** – Christian tradition and the Bible (albeit covered briefly)

3. **Skill development** – the need to think the issue through personally, the need to let God's grace shine through in all we do, and the need to discuss the issue with one another and be aware of issues around forgiveness and a past abortion.

## Areas to avoid in a talk

Avoid placing too much emphasis on images or models of foetal development. Images and descriptions of the development of a foetus in the womb may seem to be powerful tools in making a connection with the fact that life begins at conception. However, they may in fact have the opposite effect on the audience, making the whole subject appear academic and remote. Moreover, as already stated, the current worldview is that a woman's rights take precedence over that of the foetus; therefore, by grounding what is said in foetal development, a speaker can unwittingly undermine the position he or she is trying to create. Pictures might help build the case against abortion with respect to foetuses of twelve weeks, but not with respect of tiny embryos comprising two or four cells. As most theologians would agree that life begins even before that stage, I would recommend avoiding the use of images or descriptions of life in the womb during a sermon or talk on abortion.

Avoid placing too much emphasis on the psychological or physical effects of abortion. While a powerful connection with the subject can be made through the experience of men and women who go through abortion, and this is certainly a subject that needs to be mentioned, it needs to be approached with care and sensitivity. It is very important not to make general statements suggesting that all women and men 'suffer' after an abortion or are at risk of psychological problems from their involvement, even though we know that this can often be the case.

While many women and men *do* suffer painful psychological effects following an abortion, many do not. Even where such effects are present, the powerful forces of denial described earlier in the book (for example 'tunnel vision') can prevent people from understanding and acknowledging that these may be connected to their abortion.

By placing too much emphasis on the psychological effects of abortion it is possible to unintentionally alienate the majority of an audience: those who have not had an abortion will feel this is nothing to do with them, and those who are not in a place of suffering (or are in denial about their pain) may reject what is said as untrue. So while some mention of this is helpful, it is best not to make what you say dependent on the fact that these effects may be widespread.

The physical side-effects of abortion are a complex area, and perhaps best avoided altogether. While there is compelling evidence that abortion can have some negative effects, research on both sides can appear contradictory. As with images of foetal development, engaging with complex medical terms and statistical research can have the opposite effect of that intended and prove disengaging for a listener. If desired, listeners can be directed to other resources and research.

## Creating a safe environment

Tension at the beginning of a talk can be diffused with a thoughtful and sensitive introduction. The opening of the talk will set the tone, so it can help to begin with an acknowledgement that abortion is widespread in our culture and that statistically it might be a personal issue for some of those present, both men or women. This confirms to the listener that the speaker is aware that this is a very sensitive issue and that careful thought has been put into what is going to be said. If the church typically offers to pray for people at the end of a service, I would recommend specifically stating at the beginning of the talk that people will *not* be prayed for in public at the end. On our courses people tell us that when they hear abortion talked about in a service, they worry that there will be a call for prayer at the end and that they will feel they should go forward in public. This idea can be distressing for them, and so it would be helpful to put listeners at ease in this way.

## Making the connections

A bridge into the subject can be built by focusing on facts that reveal the widespread nature of abortion in our culture (as outlined in Chapter 2). Who has an abortion? Why do people experience unintended pregnancy? Why do they choose abortion? These are facts that can open minds and certainly the fact that over one third of our population experience at least one abortion comes as a complete surprise to the majority.

I have found that an effective way of drawing an audience into the subject is to describe the connection that a woman in a crisis pregnancy starts to make with the child growing in the womb before the abortion (also outlined in Chapter 2) and then to describe how for some this connection is maintained afterwards, leaving them with uncomfortable questions.

By gently describing the feelings of men and women during the crisis pregnancy and the head/heart dilemma, it is possible to start exploring what happens following an abortion. The fact that anything at all happens will come as a complete revelation to the majority of the audience (and even possibly to those who have been through abortion themselves), and they might find this concept immediately challenging and thought-provoking. The speaker does not have to make all the connections; the listeners will very quickly grasp them for themselves.

It is helpful to talk in general terms about the questions that people begin to have and the confusion that many feel after an abortion, by pointing out that to conceive is one of our deepest human instincts, and that abortion cuts across this. It is helpful to talk about the emotions that can emerge, such as confusion, anger, guilt and feelings of loss, which are accompanied by grief. Within the constraints of time, these deep emotions can only be briefly alluded to in a talk.

I believe that in this context, we should never state, or imply, that men and women can feel they have been involved in taking the life of their own child. This connection sounds judgmental and our experience on our courses has been that it is only useful to individuals if they themselves make the connection.

Overall, it is better to wrestle with the subject rather than trying to win an argument, all the time compassionately considering the position of a pregnant woman faced with the crisis of a pregnancy, and being sympathetic to her plight and the reasons why she might have chosen an abortion.

## Introducing the 'F' word: forgiveness

The subject of forgiveness should be approached with humility and sensitivity. For many men and women, just *thinking* about a past abortion might initially be too much to contemplate, let alone engaging with the issue at a deeper level. For some who have buried the memories in the 'storage box' described earlier, feelings and events can just be too painful or difficult to face or even recall.

To say, as some preachers have done, that all that is needed is a prayer of repentance, might therefore be too simplistic and unhelpful. For some, the idea of repentance and forgiveness might be a blank wall, which they have no idea how to climb over. For others it might seem a frightening prospect that is too difficult to take in. Forgiven for what? Forgiveness may even be a source of bitterness for some; surely if forgiveness is the issue, others should be asking *them* for forgiveness.

Therefore, it is more helpful to invite those who have been through abortion to explore the issue with God on their own terms and in their own time, rather than putting restraints around how this should be done (such as by asking them to confess to a sin or implying that God's grace has preconditions, for example: unless you come in repentance I will not talk to you).

It is for individuals to work out how far they want to go, and not for us to tell them. People are very different and need to be free to approach this subject in a way that is meaningful to them. What is important is that they allow the Spirit of God to guide them on their journey, and for us to work with them, possibly over a long period of time. A repentant heart and a willingness to start looking at the past honestly are more important than an over-simplistic prayer of repentance.

> "You do not delight in sacrifice, or I would bring it; you do not take pleasure in burnt offerings. The sacrifices of God are a broken spirit; a broken and contrite heart, O God, you will not despise" (Psalm 51:16–17).

## The response to the talk – what do you want your audience to do?

Encourage an audience:

1. *To respond personally to the issue.* As discussed in previous chapters, our hope is that the Christian response to this issue will be: *to resolve not to have an abortion and to live this out as an intentional value in our own lives.* This involves an understanding of the possibility of conceiving despite the use of contraception, having an open discussion with a partner on the need to welcome any new life, and as a final resort holding a positive view of adoption as a viable alternative to abortion.

2. *To respond as families.* For parents to discuss the issue themselves, and to consider discussing it with their teenagers as they grow up. It is especially important to open the doors of communication and acceptance.

3. *To respond as a congregation,* by discussing how best to establish a 'just culture', to help dispel fear of condemnation for anyone finding themselves experiencing an unintended pregnancy, and to encourage those who are struggling with past abortion experience to seek help.

I have found that the one question that nearly everyone wants to ask concerns the subject of abortion following a rape. This issue forms much of the widespread acceptance of abortion in society, and is the most frequently asked question following a talk on the subject. Questions of abortion in the case of disability of the unborn child are also often asked.

I personally believe that these questions are too complex to address in detail in a sermon, so I would recommend making further material available afterwards. I have given an answer to the difficult question based on the experience of rape within the post-abortion recovery group in Appendix I of this book. I would strongly recommend making this available as a resource afterwards. Appendix II explores the question of disability.

## The need for us all to repent

Spiritually, the roots of abortion run deep in our culture and in our churches. The fact of the matter is that many of us have not responded to the issue very well and we desperately need God's guidance and forgiveness for what is taking place in our land. There is a need to repent for the silence that has grown up in the church, and for our failure to develop an effective response. A communal act of repentance might also encourage those who have been involved to embark on a journey of personal repentance that would bring healing to our church communities. The following is a useful Scripture upon which to base an act of repentance:

> "If my people, who are called by my name, will humble themselves and pray and seek my face and turn from their wicked ways, then I will hear from heaven and will forgive their sin and will heal their land (2 Chronicles 7:14).

## Handling testimony

One consequence of breaking the silence around abortion in a church community might be women or men coming forward to offer a testimony of their personal involvement in an abortion. Post-abortion testimony is a powerful way of engaging an audience and can be a really helpful way of illustrating some of the complex effects and issues connected with abortion. However, while some testimonies are useful, others can be less so, and testifying can be difficult for someone who has not told their story in public before. There are a number of issues that require careful consideration before encouraging a public testimony to be given.

In some ways, a person who volunteers to share their story is in a vulnerable position, as they may not have fully processed their thoughts and feelings beforehand. Giving a testimony may place them under further strain, as well as adding a dimension of pressure in worrying what people may think of them afterwards.

The story that they have told themselves about events in the past may not be quite accurate, and they may benefit from an opportunity to unpack and process their memories and feelings before speaking in public. The act of giving a public testimony may make it difficult for them to change their story afterwards if they subsequently remember what actually happened more clearly.

The wrong kind of public testimony can also, paradoxically, act as a deterrent to others to seek help if they have been trying to avoid the issues caused by a past abortion. As a result, they may be put off seeking help and healing. One issue is secrecy; when someone hears a public testimony there can be a temptation to avoid the subject even further, fearing that they too will be asked to disclose their past for public scrutiny.

Some circumstances around abortion can be difficult and extreme (such as abortion following rape), and this sort of story can be unhelpful in a testimony. The average circumstance faced by most people is a man and woman from ordinary backgrounds who decide on abortion due to personal preferences. A testimony from someone with this sort of background is most useful to a listener in forging an accurate view of abortion. Stories involving a rape or medical reasons for an abortion can reinforce unhelpful stereotypes in people's minds.

If someone volunteers to give a testimony following a sermon, my advice would be to thank them and encourage them to discuss the issue thoroughly with their appointed counsellor to ensure it is dealt with fully before speaking in public. It might initially be best for them to speak in a small, confidential group such as a home group.

## Public prayer

It is good to pray about abortion – we need more prayer in this area! However, it is vital that we pray in agreement on the subject. Jesus said, "Again, I tell you that if two of you on earth agree about anything you ask for, it will be done for you by my Father in heaven. For where two or three come together in my name, there I am with them" (Mathew 18:19–20).

This would seem to imply that if we meet to pray, we need to be praying for broadly the same thing in order for our prayers to be effective. With the current diversity of opinion on abortion within the church, this may be more difficult to achieve than a leader might think, especially as people who are sympathetic to abortion tend to remain silent.

Therefore, when praying about abortion it can be helpful to try to frame a prayer in general terms with which we can all agree, taking care not to use words such as "sin" or "evil". It is also important to use language that is sensitive to the needs of those present who may have experienced abortion in their past.

For example:

> ... We pray for all those who might face a crisis pregnancy in the near future. We ask that you would be with them as they wrestle with their situation. We pray that you would send the right people to come alongside them and the right words and advice to help them. We pray you would protect them and bless them...

> ... We pray for our nation, that you would guide your church so that we have something useful to say within our congregations as well as to society as a whole. We pray that you would inspire us in creativity and insight to produce an effective apologetic that will help us reflect your truth to the wider world. We pray that we may play our part in transforming our culture so that life in all its stages becomes protected once more...

> ... We pray that men and women would learn the truth about the causes of unintended pregnancy, and how widespread the practice of abortion is in our nation. We pray that you would turn the hearts of the fathers to their children and that men and women would treat each other with love and respect...

> ... We pray for all who have been through abortion, that you would bring healing and peace to this area of their lives. We pray for more post-abortion counselling courses to become available through the church and that there would be a wider understanding of this issue among Christians...

> ... We pray that you would lift barriers of guilt and shame that might prevent people from seeking assistance and that you would restore Christians who have had abortions in your eyes and in their own eyes. We pray for all who may have lost their faith or who have felt they cannot come to church because of a past

*abortion; that you would free them from any feelings of condemnation or unworthiness and lead them back to you…*

## Summary: some suggestions for planning a sermon

*A useful theme might be suggested by Mathew 22:34–40.*

When it comes to abortion what does it mean to love the Lord our God with all your heart and all your soul and all your mind? And when it comes to abortion, what does it mean to love our neighbour as ourselves?

**Useful structure:**

1. Knowledge
2. Framework
3. Skill development

**General barriers to communication to be overcome**

- A fear that what will be said might be judgmental, or insensitive
- A disconnection that abortion is relevant to a listener's life
- Defensiveness about the political/feminist issues around abortion
- Defensiveness on the part of those who have experience of abortion, or those who have close friends or relatives who have had an abortion.

## Major on the major points

- The fact that abortion is widespread in every level of society, including among Christians
- The role of contraception in unintended pregnancy
- The fact that abortion is an issue for men as well as women
- The fact that many feel negative effects after an abortion, the memory of the pregnancy for some will maintain a strong link
- Abortion does not 'wind back the clock'
- How to form a helpful personal worldview
- The need to discuss the issue in families
- Establishing a 'just culture' in the church – what steps are you going to recommend?
- The need for corporate repentance
- An encouragement for Christians to lay past abortions at the foot of the cross.

## Minor on the academic points (these are key issues to mention, but should be kept brief)

- What the Bible says about abortion
- Theology and church history
- The 'hard' cases of rape and disability.

## Avoid completely

- Photographs of aborted foetuses

- Insensitive vocabulary
- Pro-life campaigning materials or symbols, such as tiny feet lapel pins.

**Responding afterwards**

- Ministry team prepared and organised to help those responding after a talk
- Information on post-abortion help to be given to everyone
- Information on rape and abortion
- Recommended reading list prepared.

**A word of encouragement**

I believe that preaching a sermon along the lines suggested above would be a useful part of establishing a 'just culture' in a church. However, if leaders felt that this subject was not appropriate to their Sunday teaching programme, then even holding a meeting amongst church leaders to discuss and agree the values and issues relevant to establishing a 'just culture' would be helpful. (see Chapter 8 'Where to Start'). A sermon could follow on later if desired.

# Chapter 7

## Pastoral care in the local church

### Meeting with someone who wishes to discuss a past abortion

If we begin to talk about abortion with compassion and relevance in our churches, people may come forward wishing to talk through their involvement in a past abortion. This chapter is based on our experience of meeting with people as we talk about our work in churches, and what we have found to be helpful in this situation. It has been written for people who have a pastoral role within a church, and includes suggestions for how to help those who respond immediately following a talk in the church, and those who need on-going support and counselling. It assumes that the person wishing to discuss the issue is a committed Christian, and that prayer will form part of the counselling process.

I would recommend that before starting any post-abortion counselling or prayer it would be helpful to have in place a mechanism of supervision or referral should more specialised counselling be required.

## 1. The first meeting

### Sensitivity and confidentiality

First, thought should be given to the immediate issue of confidentiality in a church setting, and where the initial discussion might take place. Some people might be comfortable talking when there are other people in the vicinity, but others may feel acutely sensitive to being seen or overheard and would welcome being taken to a more private place to talk. Ideally, men should talk to men and women to women. We have found that making arrangements by email, and giving people permission to use an alias or assumed first name can give confidence that confidentiality will be respected.

As have already seen, there is a lot of secrecy surrounding abortion, thus making it a very sensitive issue, so personal stories revealed should be treated as highly confidential, and not discussed in any way with others (with the obvious exception of counselling supervision or safety issues). Tremendous damage can be caused in the creation of a 'just culture' if people are aware that counselling for abortion is taking place, even if an individual is not specifically named.

This may be the first time that someone has shared their experience with anyone, and your initial and subsequent reactions will be vitally important to them. Affirm them and thank them for telling you. If you see them subsequently, do not avoid or ignore them in company, unless they wish to avoid you. They will be sensitive and watching for possible rejection.

### Time

We have already noted the significance of the step those responding have taken, and this should be acknowledged by giving them sufficient time. It may be that on this first occasion (for example at the end of a service), members of the pastoral team have limited time, and so a further appointment should be made to talk further.

### Listen

Some may find it difficult to know where to begin in sharing their story, especially if they have kept their experience a secret. They may be struggling to remember details of what happened, and will need you to help them by asking sensitive questions. They may want to know what you personally think about abortion, and it would be good for members of the pastoral team to have thought this through for themselves. You should avoid being drawn into agreeing with their decision for abortion, despite the circumstances. A balance of grace and truth is hard to achieve, but this will ultimately be of help to them.

The following are helpful questions to ask:

- Who else have you told? What was their reaction?
- Why do you think you are looking at this now?
- What happened? When? Why?
- Did you have any other abortions?

Your role in this meeting is not to try to bring this person to a point of resolution; it is not to try and 'fix' the situation. Your role should be to try to discern what the Holy Spirit is doing in their life by bringing them to you, and to help them as far as they want to be helped and are willing to go.

People are very different and have varying needs and approaches to resolving the issue of a past abortion. On their journey towards healing, some will wish to discuss the circumstances of the abortion itself, while others will be resolving a tangle of events, emotions and attitudes. Therefore, it is extremely important to try not to impose your resolution on the situation, even if an answer seems obvious to you. Allow the individual concerned to make their own connections in their own time.

### Prayer

It is best not to rush into suggesting a prayer of forgiveness for those seeking help, as this may not be appropriate for everyone. We need to listen and ask what they want to do. God loves men and women who have had abortions; it is not an unforgivable sin from which there is no redemption. As we talk to someone who has had an abortion, we should try to set aside our own judgment and feelings and wait on God to see where he would like to lead. Suggested ways to introduce the topic of repentance and forgiveness will be mentioned later.

## 2. Ongoing support

For some, this initial meeting may be all that they require and it may be the end of the process, but for others it may be a beginning. Invite them back, leaving the door open for them to return as they process their thoughts and feelings. Think about how to provide ongoing support and discuss this with them. More in-depth support may be available through organisations such as CareConfidential, or professional Christian counsellors.

Within the context of the local church there are two areas that might be helpful to cover: accountability and forgiveness.

## Accountability

One of the stages of our post-abortion course focuses on accountability. Participants are asked to identify all whom they felt were involved in their abortion experience. Then, in the form of a pie chart, they allocate proportions of responsibility for the abortion decision. This is a very personal exercise. Its purpose is not to shift the blame onto others, but to try to draw out (from what are sometimes very complicated situations) the extent of each person's own accountability towards God.

Before doing this exercise, it is not uncommon for many women or men to take all of the responsibility for the decision made, or conversely, to put it all on their partner. The truth of the matter is that abortion is a common practice in our culture and acceptance of it is widespread. Many people are involved in each abortion, from medical professionals and abortion counsellors, to those involved in education and making our laws. Parents and friends can sometimes play a key part, and an individual's own attitudes and values are also relevant.

Making a list of all those who are accountable and involved can be a strangely liberating experience for someone being counselled and can help them see their situation realistically. It helps them to sort out in their own minds what they need to take to God in repentance, and where they need to forgive others and let things go.

There are two mistakes that those being counselled can make: one is taking too little responsibility, and the other is taking too much. If they take on too little responsibility, forgiveness will not work. If they take on too much, then they are taking on the sins of others and will not feel forgiven at the end of the process. Rather than definitive answers, what is needed is a willingness to engage with the issues and wrestle with them honestly.

### Forgiveness

While it is entirely possible for some people to repent quickly and simply for an abortion and to move on, others might find it more complicated and, as already stated, may need to process thoughts and feelings from the past in order to resolve the issue. This is a legitimate way of resolving the issue and it is important that people are free to do this if that is what they feel is needed.

If someone approaches you asking for help, they are probably struggling and not getting the answers they need. At the heart of the issue lies the question of what has actually been lost. Some can face this question and their involvement, but others may not be able to.

The key here is the ministry of the Holy Spirit and his ability to prise open gaps in the past, in which you can pray for the Holy Spirit to do his work. When someone is genuinely 'stuck', a good place to start is where they are now. What do they feel and think *now*? What connections *are* they able to make? Then work backwards towards the abortion remembering events along the way, rather than starting with the pregnancy and trying to work forwards, which would be the more obvious way of approaching the subject.

For some, a simple prayer asking for forgiveness will be like a life-giving stream of water found in the desert; thirsted after, eagerly sought and welcomed. But for others the idea of repentance and forgiveness is too difficult to take in and work out.

The idea of forgiveness may even be a source of anger or bitterness for some: they may feel others should be asking them for forgiveness, rather than the other way round. Therefore, it may be difficult to come to a place where they can resolve the issues and feel forgiven themselves.

The key to forgiveness is effective repentance. A good way of looking at repentance is this: "Rewind the video, if you were back there would you do something different? Was it just a mistake or something you feel responsible for?" If this is too difficult due to complex circumstances, perhaps a better question to ask is: "Knowing what you do now, would you do something different now if you were in similar circumstances, for example exploring the possibility of giving birth or adoption as an alternative to abortion?" Resolving to change ingrained attitudes or behaviours can sometimes be the key to receiving God's forgiveness.

Useful questions to help explore this are:

- What were the reasons you found yourself in the circumstances that you did?
- Are you still engaged in any behaviours that contributed to those circumstances?
- Is there anything that you need to change in your life to ensure that another abortion does not happen?

I have met with people who are frustrated and left feeling inadequate because a counsellor has implied that they should have moved on by now. Equally, I have met with others who resent any implication that they have dealt with the issue too lightly. Everyone is different and discernment and sensitivity are required.

Forgiveness can be a process. It might need to be worked at!

At an appropriate point you might consider a formal confession service. The sacrament of Communion holds real power and can be very helpful to a committed Christian. Whether it is the beginning of a process, the end of a process or dealing with one stage of the process, Communion can help cut the deep and unhelpful spiritual ties that bind people to a past abortion and I would recommend using this during your time together. Some denominations have a formal confession; I personally use the *Book of Common Prayer* (the contemporary version is called *Common Worship* and has a very good service of confession called "Reconciliation").

## Confronting the loss

As mentioned earlier, many women and men make a connection in their minds that leads them to think they have participated in ending the life of their child. This connection can be a key part of healing, although it is clearly a difficult area. However, it is only useful to the person being counselled if they themselves are the one who makes this connection. Therefore, it is important that a counsellor does not attempt to make this connection for them through discussing the loss of their child. This is a subject that they themselves should bring up and discover. So, while it might be helpful to assist them in exploring any general feelings of loss, it is best not to suggest the root or cause of these feelings.

## Moving On

For the team of helpers on our courses our greatest reward is to see the transformation that takes place in the women and men over the course of just a few weeks. Most achieve a liberation that produces an extraordinary inner glow, although some do not appear to have quite resolved the issue.

Occasionally, we meet some of the people who did not appear to make progress on the course a few months or years afterwards. Some come rushing up and thank us for the course, telling us that it has transformed their lives. So even if those met with do not appear to resolve the issue, I would encourage counsellors to persist and continue praying for them after your time together. You do not know what is going on under the surface and most seem to get there in the end. It just takes time.

If you are reading this book and a past abortion is a personal issue for you, I would also encourage you if your feeling is that not everyone needs to go on a course. If someone has resolved the issue and laid it before God in the privacy of his or her own home that is fine. Others feel that they might need to look at deeper issues that would have been difficult to identify and confront on their own. If you are reading this chapter and have a personal experience of abortion ask yourself: how you feel now? If you are at peace with your experience, please go in peace. Need to look at something? Get in touch with your local prayer counselling team, or a Christian counsellor. It could be a life-changing experience!

# Chapter 8

## Breaking the silence in the church

There is a need to open up and debate the practice of abortion that occurs among Christians today. As a church we need to do this before we reach out to help those with an unplanned pregnancy or who are in pain from a past abortion. We need to be in the best position we can in order to listen, offer advice and pray for people in these situations.

Within our culture there is pressure to view the practice of abortion as the only positive option. Balancing this is the silence around what happens to many after an abortion, and lack of knowledge of the genuinely empowering alternatives, which are rarely discussed. By continuing the silence around the subject of abortion within the church, Christians unwittingly continue the silence about the after effects of abortion and fail to promote a positive view of the other options for an unplanned pregnancy.

Therefore, it is helpful for Christians today to engage with the subject to understand the risks and take steps to avoid them. On our courses we have seen good Christian men and women of all ages from many different denominations and Christian traditions abort their children because they were unprepared for what life threw at them. Recently we have seen several young couples who had abortions early in their marriages because a child did not fit into their plans. We have seen the children of church leaders who couldn't talk with their parents about unplanned pregnancy, and couples who could not face a late pregnancy. Many times we hear heart-breaking stories of godly women or men who have a momentary slip that ends with an unplanned pregnancy. Unless something is done, this situation will continue.

## Where to start?

It is not uncommon to hear sermons about drug and alcohol addiction, sexual abuse, homelessness, divorce and single parent families, tithing, sex before marriage, parenting skills or relationships. I believe that it is time to start discussing the subject of unplanned pregnancy – within and outside marriage – among Christians, discussing the real choices that are available and the consequences of those choices.

In the current status quo it may never feel right to begin speaking about abortion. It may feel uncomfortable to schedule a sermon on the subject in the church, or to raise it in youth and student groups. It might be difficult for a leader to imagine raising the issue with a church's governing body. It may be difficult for a leader to imagine that members of their congregation have had abortions in the past. Therefore, breaking the silence in our churches needs a high degree of intentionality on the part of church leaders to initiate a vision for change, even if that change is quite small.

I believe that there are two simple steps that could facilitate the necessary action: first, developing a consensus among leaders of a church as to the issues and how abortion should be thought about and discussed with sensitivity; and second, communicating these values to the wider membership, either through discussion of the issue or a sermon on the subject along the lines suggested in Chapter 6. If a sermon or formal talk is not desired, delivering a short statement in public affirming the values that you have agreed amongst yourselves in the creation of a 'just culture' might be helpful. There is also a considerable power in word-of-mouth communication, especially among female members of a congregation, where I have observed a real desire to know and understand this issue.

A leadership meeting or seminar to develop such a consensus could include:

- Information on abortion statistics: who has an abortion, why do they get pregnant, what happens to them afterwards?

- An acknowledgement of the real risk of both unintended pregnancy and abortion to Christians

- A short review of traditional Christian teaching

- The importance of compassion and helpful language

- The values that you wish to promote around unconditional acceptance of someone with an unplanned pregnancy or someone who has an abortion in their past

- How to pray through the issue of a past abortion with someone who asks for this.

Even if no statement is delivered in public, just discussing and agreeing these matters amongst leaders would be an important step forwards in the creation and promotion of a 'just culture'. They say values are caught not taught. If leaders find the courage to engage with this difficult issue and develop a consensus amongst a leadership team, gradually this will begin to have an effect.

In the current silence, unhelpful teaching or the influence of a few with extreme views can hold a disproportionate sway. I estimate a very small percentage of Christians have an active, traditional pro-life view, but while many of the holders of these values are good, godly men and women, sometimes the vocabulary and presentation can achieve the opposite of that intended, and can actually be quite unhelpful. Unless such language is firmly rebutted by leaders it can become, by default, the basis of a culture of judgment and condemnation around the issue within a church. It is important to fill the vacuum that currently surrounds the subject with teaching that is compassionate, helpful and understanding.

I do understand that saying *anything* about abortion might appear daunting to church leaders who may never have heard anything constructive said on the subject. If it seems too difficult to know where to start, my advice and encouragement is to start by prayerfully discussing this with a small number of other leaders.

## Reaching out to a hurting world: a vision for post-abortion counselling.

Martin Luther King said:

> "There was a time when the church was very powerful. It was during that period when the early Christians rejoiced when

they were deemed worthy to suffer for what they believed. In those days the church was not merely a thermometer that recorded the ideas and principals of popular opinion; it was a thermostat that transformed the mores [morals] of society."[41]

I believe that by implementing the above steps Christians could begin to find confidence in their values and thus start to influence the surrounding culture, and start to function as a thermostat rather than a thermometer. Perhaps the greatest opportunity for Christians lies in the area of post-abortion counselling, where there is a great need to bring compassion, healing and restoration to those hurting from a past abortion. This is just the area that plays to the traditional Christian strengths of love, compassion and pastoral care, and in which Christians could be most effective.

When I first asked if I could start a post-abortion course at a church in London, the leaders were puzzled by my request. They thought that it might be better to start a crisis pregnancy counselling service, which might help women considering abortion change their minds, or help those wishing to keep their children. I appreciate that a post-abortion course might have seemed counterintuitive and not the most obvious course of action, but when I stuck to my request they graciously assented and we have been running the courses ever since.

By listening to those who have experienced abortion, I have learnt that abortion is a reflection of the deeply-held values and complex behaviour of those within our culture. Challenging the idea that abortion is the most helpful outcome for a woman with an unplanned pregnancy therefore requires an understanding of this behaviour and what happens after an abortion. I believe that understanding the connections that women and men make with their children lost through an abortion adds a dimension to our thinking, shows us the hidden complexities, and can challenge the casual acceptance of abortion by our society. This is an area where the church can play to its strengths, and perhaps one day become the thermostat that reduces the number of abortions in society as a whole.

## Creating alternative support structures

Filmmaker Julia Black, who filmed an entire abortion for a television documentary, said that she wished to challenge our 'lazy' thinking on the subject.[42] If we are serious about reducing the number of abortions in our society we need to create alternative support structures that offer women genuine choice. This may require effort and imagination, but it would certainly be better than pressurising women into something that many say afterwards they did not really want.

For example, although the adoption system is now light years away from what it used to be, we remain stuck with hostile and unduly negative attitudes towards adoption. Does the system really meet the needs of women today? Is it really a realistic choice for a woman in this position? When was the last time anybody asked women what they really want from the adoption process?

A creative example of an alternative structure supporting birth mothers is provided by the *We Are Family* project, set up in 2005 by Alternatives Crisis Pregnancy Centre in the East End of London. The project acts as a catalyst to help single mothers and provides emotional and practical support, life skills and parenting skills, to those with no wider family support structure. It is this sort of initiative that could come naturally to church communities once the silence around abortion is broken.

The assumption underpinning the promotion of abortion as the solution to unintended pregnancy is that it is something that many women will automatically want; that it will nearly always be the preferred *'choice'*.

What about women who would rather be pregnant? What do they want? Might large numbers of women actually want to experience pregnancy, to be pregnant and to give birth, but feel unable to do so in a society that only offers abortion as a viable alternative? Could this be the reason for the high rate of pregnancy and subsequent abortion, and the high rate of repeat abortions? Perhaps creating new, imaginative support structures that encourage women to give birth and men to support their choice would empower women in their lives in a way that abortion does not. The message that can come across to some pregnant women is that they are undervalued and viewed as useless. As a society we are not prepared to offer them real choices.

Having an informed view is about engaging with the down side of abortion. It is about the reality that abortion leaves many women living with the nihilistic thought, *"I have participated in ending the life of my own child."* It is about understanding the dynamics of contraception and the high risk of pregnancy. It is about creating structures that enable women to be pregnant when they want to be and empower their choices. It is about giving women a real choice. It is about pregnant women feeling valued and protected.

## An inspiring story

Margaret O'Hara led one of our courses. On this course there was a Saturday session and for this Margaret invited us to her home, and then to go with her to her local church the next day. As we drove down the hill to the church, one of the women said, "Wait, I know this place, I've been here before." She told of how many years previously, she had been in great turmoil when she discovered she was pregnant. She was the daughter of a senior church leader and was a committed Christian herself.

At the time of her pregnancy she felt that she could not talk to her father about it in case it put him in a difficult position. As she was thinking about having an abortion, she was driving along a motorway when she saw the spire of a church and pulled off at the next junction to find the church and pray about her situation. She entered the church building and as she started to pray she felt God tell her not to have the abortion. But she went ahead and had been carrying the guilt for many years.

The church Margaret took us to was the very same one the young woman had stopped to pray in all those years ago. She was filled with an unspeakable joy that spoke to her of absolute redemption and restoration. That God should lead her back to the same place gave her a personal reassurance that he had been with her all the time; that he had never let her go in spite of what she had done. When we met up the following week her face shone with absolute radiance. Here was a woman at peace!

This is just one story of God's grace towards a woman who had an abortion. It shows us where God is in the abortion debate: alongside those who are having abortions, calling them to choose differently beforehand, but ready to pick up the pieces afterwards. It also shows us where the church could be: standing alongside pregnant women as they wrestle with their situation and choices, and being there with arms outstretched whatever decision they make.

Our ministry of post-abortion recovery works because at its centre is the hope and reconciliation found in Jesus Christ. He is at the heart of everything we do and only through him is full healing and restoration possible. This is why the church has such a vital role to play and why it could be so effective in offering this truth to our society, thus bringing about real change. This will not come through campaigning, or judging those who have been through abortion, but by communicating effectively, living out true values in our own lives and by bringing God's love to those in need. This is the model that could form our response to the issue.

# Appendix I

## Rape and abortion

Questions around rape and abortion are highly charged and difficult to discuss without raising strong feelings. However, great though the temptation is to avoid the subject, I have noticed whenever speaking about our work in youth or church groups this is the one question that is nearly always asked, people really want to know about and discuss this issue.

In our post-abortion groups we encountered women for whom this had been their experience, and we have ended up with a slightly different take on the issue. As with the wider picture of abortion, I think the best place to start thinking this through is to understand what is going on in our society.

A crime survey published in 2007[43] revealed the true extent of the horror of rape perpetrated against women in England and Wales. This authoritative and comprehensive study revealed that one in 20 women have been raped since the age of sixteen. One in 200 had been raped in the previous year. In terms of the population of England and Wales, 85,000 women are raped each year, equivalent to an average of 230 per day. This survey shows how the true extent of this crime is far greater than the officially reported figures of 11,000[44] for the same year (2007), or similar numbers of 14,000[45] for the most recent figures in 2010–11. Rape is a consistently underreported and hidden crime, and is widespread at many levels of our society.

Therefore, it is highly likely that a significant number of pregnancies and subsequent abortions take place as a result of rape every year.[46] Most people believe that in these circumstances the option of abortion should be available to women, and this decision has wide support in our culture. However, on our post-abortion recovery courses, a number of issues raised in connection with rape and abortion challenged my conventional thinking on the subject, leading me to suggest that they merit serious consideration. Counter-intuitively, some women who have been pregnant following a rape can come to feel that abortion is not necessarily the best option. This view has been expressed by some of the women who attended our course, who had been subject to rape (but not all).

Perhaps this important point can start to be explored by relating the experience of two women who were rape survivors (but who had not become pregnant or experienced abortion) who attended one of our first groups. It was interesting for them to hear the stories of those who had been through abortion, and they both benefited greatly from being on the course. (They attended the course at the invitation of one of the leaders, who felt that they would benefit, given their lack of access to post-rape counselling.)

At the end, one of the women said, "I had always assumed that had I got pregnant as a result of my rape I would have had an abortion.

But having heard these women's experiences I can now say that I would definitely not have an abortion, even as a result of being raped. It would be like being raped twice."

Why did she say that? What was it about what she had heard that made her change her mind?

A woman who has conceived as a result of being raped is being asked to make a hasty decision about an abortion under pressure and in dramatic circumstances, which have been forced upon her. She will be suffering from trauma and might find thinking about the present very difficult, let alone thinking about what might be best for her and what she might want for the future.

Although abortion appears to be a simple procedure, in this book we have considered the possible complications many women experience, which could add to the trauma of the rape. One of the course leaders reflected on her experience of counselling women who had been through rape and abortion saying: "In choosing an abortion, you are not choosing whether to have the baby or not to have the baby. You are choosing between having the baby and having a traumatic experience. So on top of being raped it is choosing another traumatic experience."

In their book *Victims and Victors*, David Reardon, Julie Makimaa and Amy Sobie contrast a number of testimonies from women who have been in this position:

- Patricia, who was drugged and raped, became pregnant and had an abortion: "The effects of the abortion are much more far-reaching than the effects of the rape in my life" (Patricia Ryan).[47]

- Rebecca was raped by a friend and became pregnant. Following an abortion she said, "They say abortion is the easy way out, the best thing for everyone, but they are wrong. It has been over fifteen years and I still suffer" (Rebecca Morris).[48]

- Helene, who was raped during her first year at college, stated, "Abortion does not help or solve a problem, it only compounds and creates another trauma for the already grieving victim by taking away the one thing that can bring joy" (Helene Evans).[49]

It is commonly assumed that rape victims who become pregnant would naturally want an abortion, but that is not necessarily always the case. Some may want to keep their child. To my knowledge there are no surveys available in Britain showing whether women who conceive as a result of rape wish to give birth to their children. However, one study in the US found just over 50% of rape victims decided to continue with the pregnancy, with 32% deciding to keep their children, 6% releasing their child for adoption and 12% experiencing a miscarriage.[50]

Many women do not agree with abortion, and some victims of assault become introspective[51]; their sense of the value of life and respect for others is heightened, and to have an abortion would go against this. Others believe that if they can get through the pregnancy they will have conquered the rape: giving birth is proof that they are better than the rapist as, while he was selfish, she can be generous.

This statement from Makimaa and Sobie's book is particularly compelling. They tell the story of Kathleen who was brutally raped and decided to place her child for adoption. During the pregnancy she changed her mind and decided to keep the child, "Once the baby continued to kick and move, I began to have different feelings towards the child. I began to realise that this little life inside of me was struggling too. Somehow my heart changed" (Kathleen DeZeeuw)[52]

Cindy was raped by a neighbour but decided to keep her child, "Through our children we begin to see more clearly what love and sacrifice are all about. To give life is to receive life in all its fullness" (Cindy Speltz)[53]

As explained earlier, our society tends to think that by making abortion available, a woman who becomes pregnant following rape has real choices. But is this true? It may look compassionate, but what is the alternative? Where can a pregnant rape survivor go to be looked after while she decides what to do with her future? Where can she receive specialist counselling and support? Where is the place of security and anonymity where she could be loved and cared for during her pregnancy if she decides she would like to keep her child?

Where can a woman who comes from a culture in which discovery of a rape would result in her exclusion or persecution find shelter during her pregnancy, allowing her to rebuild her life on her own terms? Where is the adoption system adapted for the specific needs of women who have been raped and who wish to take time deciding on their future options, to see how they might feel about the child once it is born? Would it make a difference if it were a boy or a girl for instance? There is pain in releasing a child for adoption, but from our experience on the post-abortion course, pain can also be caused by the guilt and trauma of an abortion.

Rape is about taking away a woman's choice, so I would suggest that the care and support that a woman is offered following a rape needs to be empowering. Although most people would understand that a woman in this position might choose to have an abortion, to assume automatically that this is in her best interests, or what she would always want is to inflict another wrong on someone to whom a great injustice has already been inflicted.

Many assume that a woman who has been raped might want an abortion because if she gave birth, she would be reminded of the rape every time she looked at the child, and that was certainly the reason why some of the rape victims on our course chose abortion. But what people in general may not see is that a woman aborting a child conceived by rape is not just aborting the product of the rape; she is also aborting a deep part of her own motherhood, thus adding a further level of pain and potential trauma to the rape itself. Women wanting to keep their children can also come up against another hidden prejudice:

> "Because the actual experiences of pregnant sexual assault victims have not been widely heard, the social myth that abortion is the best, or even the only, option in cases of rape pregnancies is almost universally accepted. This universal myth creates its own set of problems for women. When a pregnant sexual assault victim balks at having an abortion, she will almost immediately faces queries of suspicion from family and friends. How can any woman have a rapist's child, they wonder? And then the suspicion mounts . . . maybe she lied. Maybe she was not really the victim of a 'legitimate' rape? And so the assumption that surely a real rape victim would want an abortion creates a new pressure on hurting women, in a time

of intense crisis, to accept the recommendation of abortion, despite moral qualms and heightened sensitivity to victimization, to swallow their reservations and have the abortion if only to silence the rising doubts about their rape story."[54]

Of the two hundred women that we have counselled, approximately ten had their abortions due to rape. Reflecting on their experiences, Nicky-Sue said this about rape and abortion:

"Something that would be helpful here in considering whether abortion is right after a rape is to answer the question backwards, as it were. One of the women who came on the course who had had an abortion as the result of rape worked through the course alongside her group and found absolutely everything on the course to be entirely relevant to her. She dealt with exactly the same emotional issues and exactly the same thought processes.

"The decision making might have been a little different; there were, perhaps in her own mind, a few more arguments in favour of abortion for her, but the impact of the abortion was exactly the same. I think that in itself is an answer. She was as much a victim of the abortion as the rape. Of course, it is up to an individual woman to decide what she can stand, but a woman does not feel less guilt for having an abortion after being raped, she does not feel less grief following an abortion after she has been raped; it's exactly the same. After the powerful experience of being raped, the impact of abortion can be doubled in its effect really, because she sees it as something that was ultimately damaging to her. That has been helpful to me in my thinking and perhaps that is helpful for you too."

Some of the situations and stories we hear in the post-abortion healing group are simply terrible. Truly awful things can happen to women in our society through absolutely no fault of their own. But the heartbreak and distress of abortion is also more awful than is realised. There are no simple answers, no convenient solutions.

The challenge and opportunity is for the church and Christian organisations to fill the gap: to provide that place of shelter and love where women who have had a terrible wrong inflicted upon them can be protected and empowered to find the help and access to the services they need, at a time of their own choosing. They could be offered a place that will give them the space and time to decide whether they want to continue with the pregnancy, and possibly consider adoption for the baby, or to have an abortion. Whatever they choose, they will need help to rebuild their lives.

# Appendix II

## Disability, pre-natal screening and abortion

Central to the widespread acceptance of abortion in our culture is the situation where a disability has been identified during pregnancy, and a woman or a couple feel they could not cope with the situation. Approximately 2,000 abortions take place every year for this reason,[55] which represents around 1% of the total. This is a significant number and a very real and devastating dilemma for a great number of people.

As Christians, what should our response be as we consider this issue? How can we approach the subject in a way that might be of help to a woman or a couple who wish to enter into a screening programme (including foetal scanning), or to those who are entering a genetic counselling process prior to becoming pregnant? I believe that insights from the post-abortion counselling groups can bring a useful perspective.

## Pre-natal screening during pregnancy

*Before considering the issue of pre-natal screening and testing, it should be stressed that if, during a pregnancy, a medical practitioner advises a test that is aimed at protecting the health of mother and child, their advice should be taken.*

Access to genetic information has increased enormously in the past few years. Pre-natal testing and screening procedures are becoming ever more accurate and sophisticated. In advanced industrial countries, pre-natal testing for detecting foetal abnormalities has become routine, so it is highly likely that a pregnant woman in the West will be offered an array of different screening options, from scans and blood tests to more invasive procedures such as amniocentesis or Chorionic Villus Sampling (CVS).

This is an issue, therefore, that every woman or couple needs to think about carefully when a pregnancy has begun, because virtually every pregnant woman in the UK will be offered some form of pre-natal screening, including a pre-natal scan.

One might assume that this is a process designed to provide reassurance to a pregnant mother or couple. However, I would suggest that the medical reality is that screening tests are offered in order to make abortion available as an option should an abnormality be detected.

While in a very small number of cases it might be possible to intervene medically if a problem were discovered, for the overwhelming majority of cases where an abnormality is detected, a termination of the pregnancy would be offered. It is important to understand that although pre-natal scanning can produce wonderful images of life growing in the womb – images that perhaps reassure a pregnant mother and help her bond with her baby – those undertaking the scanning process are often looking for abnormalities. It could be said that by agreeing to a scan, one is de facto entering into a screening process.

By the time most abnormalities are detected, a pregnancy will probably be in the second or third trimester (more than fourteen weeks), which is late for an abortion, and so a medical professional would almost certainly recommend that if a decision for abortion is to be made, it should be made as soon as possible, perhaps even the same day as the diagnosis.

The pressure to reach a hasty decision can turn what is a stressful situation into one of panic. Therefore, it would be helpful for anyone embarking on pre-natal testing (including a foetal scan) to think through its possible implications, and to discuss the matter of abortion with a partner in advance of any situation where it might become a possibility.

Being presented with the devastating news that a wanted child will have a disability must turn a woman or couple's world upside down in an instant and leave them fearful for the future. The prospect of bringing a child into the world where the odds are stacked against them might just seem too difficult to bear, and the responsibility of making such a decision could seem almost more painful than choosing abortion. It is easy to see how an abortion could appear to be the kindest thing for all concerned, both in the interests of parents and the child, and possibly also for any other children. It can be hard enough to raise able-bodied children and the world can seem an unforgiving place. But is abortion really in the best interests of those concerned?

As discussed at length in earlier chapters, our perspective from the post-abortion counselling course is that abortion does not wind back the clock and there can be unexpected consequences to an abortion. Where a disability has been discovered several weeks into a pregnancy, there could be an added level of complication because a mother has had time to bond with her baby at a deeper level and the child has become precious and wanted.

The pressure to have an abortion might be perceived as something that is being forced upon her by outside circumstances rather than originating from within, leading to a powerful feeling of coercion and loss of control, even though it is actually the woman (or the couple) who makes the decision.

At the heart of a diagnosis of abnormality or disability lies a quite understandable fear: fear of the future and what a disability might mean. My advice to anyone in this position would be to take time and not to make an abortion decision in haste. Facing our fears can sometimes help dispel them. There are many specialised support groups that can offer help and advice, and ultimately for parents who felt they could not cope there might be the alternative of adoption.

As Christians we believe, and may have heard preached, that where a disability has been diagnosed during pregnancy, the foetus is still a human being and therefore has a right to life. However, we all have our limitations and do not know how we may respond to such a challenge. Legalistic language is not helpful to a woman where an abnormality has been diagnosed, and people in this situation need encouragement to take life one step at a time and to receive the help and support they might need. They could be invited to look at the possibility of adoption (depending on what has been diagnosed) in the event that they could not cope, thus being offered a genuine choice in this situation, which might help to lift the burden of responsibility and encourage parents to continue with the pregnancy.

Women especially in this situation need unconditional love, even if there is talk of an abortion, and the support of our churches in offering more practical support and ministries for those with physical and mental disabilities. My godmother, Mary Straw, runs a house church in Montreal (the Julia Kraft Centre) for those with severe mental disabilities. She struggles to form links and to receive support from local churches because her ministry just does not fit in with traditional structures. Perhaps this is a gap in our model of doing church. If we are to be serious about challenging the widespread cultural acceptance of abortion in the case of disability, perhaps we are the ones who should be doing the rethinking in terms of engaging with those who have different needs.

## Genetic counselling prior to becoming pregnant

Genetic counselling can be helpful for people who are concerned about a specific genetic disease. It normally involves a short-term educational process for individuals and families at risk of a genetic disease, those who have a family history of a genetic disease, or those who are considering genetic testing. Genetic counsellors are trained healthcare professionals with experience in medical genetics, ethics, healthcare and counselling. They are trained to help families understand genetic disorders and provide information and support to those families.

There are a variety of circumstances that may lead someone to seek advice from a genetic counsellor. For those at risk of having a baby with a disorder, genetic counselling can help:

- Assess the risk of genetic disorders by researching their family history for any genetic diseases;

- Weigh the medical and ethical issues of genetic testing;

- Decide if they should undergo carrier testing before pregnancy;

- Decide if they should become pregnant;

- Decide if they should have pre-natal testing;

- Interpret the results of the testing;

- Explain possible treatments or preventative measures for genetic diseases.

While genetic counselling can be a process that might dispel fear and help assess risk, it is important for individuals, especially Christians, to work out their views on abortion prior to entering into the genetic counselling process, and to make it clear to a counsellor if abortion is not an option for them.

It is especially important to ask what pre-natal tests might be offered during a pregnancy and if any treatments would be available if a condition were present. Some diagnostic tests present a risk of miscarriage (for example amniocentesis or Chorionic Villus Sampling (CVS)), and although these tests might offer reassurance during pregnancy, I have had conversations with distraught parents who have miscarried following such tests. If abortion is off the list of options it might be best to question the value of invasive testing once a pregnancy has begun.

## Summary

It may be hard for some of us to think of life with a disability as desirable, and on one television programme debating the subject of euthanasia I heard a severely disabled person stating that they wished they had never been born. But I do not believe that this is the case for the overwhelming majority of people born with disabilities, many of whom live full and fascinating lives. While it is tempting in Christian circles to point to such giants as Nick Vujicic, who was born without arms or legs and preaches to millions of people around the world, the overwhelming majority of people with disabilities will lead ordinary, but wholly worthwhile and fulfilling lives. Each and every one of us remains precious in God's eyes from conception to death.

# Appendix III

## Are there psychological risks to an abortion?

Controversy has long raged between organisations providing abortion services and critics who assert that there are significant psychological risks associated with abortion.

At the heart of the difficulty in making an objective analysis lies the problem of following up case studies of a sufficient number of women who have had abortions, for a sufficient length of time, to be able to draw a significant conclusion. Psychological and emotional problems following abortion are widely reported, and many of those experiencing them link these problems directly to their abortions. The perceived wisdom among abortion providers is that reported problems are an indication of pre-existing or latent conditions that preceded the abortion.

For example, the conclusion of a 2004 report from the Royal College of Obstetricians and Gynaecologists into the care of women following an abortion sums up the situation like this:

"Psychological sequelae [effects]: some studies suggest that rates of psychiatric illness or self-harm are higher among women who have had an abortion compared with women who give birth and to non-pregnant women of similar age. It must be borne in mind that these findings do not imply a causal association and may reflect continuation of pre-existing conditions."[56]

A 2011 update to this report stated the view that:

"Women with an unintended pregnancy should be informed that the evidence suggests that they are no more or less likely to suffer adverse psychological sequelae whether they have an abortion or continue with the pregnancy and have the baby."[57]

But a study undertaken by Priscilla Coleman, Professor of Human Development and Family Studies at Bowling Green University, Ohio, has thrown new light on the subject. Endorsed by the Royal College of Psychiatrists and published in the British Journal of Psychiatry,[58] her peer-reviewed study was based on the analysis of 22 projects, which altogether analysed the experiences of 877,000 women of whom 163,831 had had an abortion. Her findings showed that:

- Women who had undergone an abortion experienced an 81% higher risk of mental health problems;

- Nearly 10% of the incidence of all mental health problems were shown to be directly attributable to abortion;

- Abortion is linked to an increased chance of anxiety disorders (34%) and depression (37%);

- Abortion is linked to a 110% higher risk of alcohol abuse, 220% higher risk of cannabis use and a 155% higher risk of suicidal behaviour.

Professor Coleman said, "There are in fact some real risks associated with abortion that should be shared with women as they are counselled prior to an abortion."[59]

This study (the latest in a long line of highly credible academic studies warning of significant risks) seems to indicate that there is indeed a psychological or emotional price to be paid after having an abortion. Crucially, the study also found that women who experienced an unplanned pregnancy and had the baby were significantly less likely to have mental health problems than similar women who aborted unplanned pregnancies. According to the study, women with a history of abortion were 55% more likely to have mental health problems than women who did not abort the pregnancy.

## Is this issue significant?

Expert opinion is divided as to the existence of a direct link between abortion and mental health problems. What are we to make of this issue? Is it a significant one for those thinking of having an abortion or for those who have had an abortion?

Aside from the fact that it would be a good idea for someone going for an abortion to have all the information available, this issue is important because one of the founding pillars of society's acceptance of abortion is the assumption that abortion is *good* for the mental health and wellbeing of women: that it will relieve the distress and mental anguish of women in a crisis pregnancy, and will be less stressful or damaging than giving birth to an unplanned or unintended child.[60]

Acknowledging that abortion carries increased and potentially life-changing psychological or emotional risks fundamentally undermines the assumption that an abortion is automatically a better option than childbirth for the mental and emotional wellbeing of a woman.

In September 2011, British MP Nadine Dorries attempted to pass a motion in the House of Commons requiring abortion providers to give those seeking an abortion access to independent counselling. Such counselling would include provision for a full, independent disclosure of the risks of an abortion procedure, including the potential psychological and emotional risks. Ms Dorries claimed that such a provision would drastically reduce the number of abortions, but the motion was defeated in the House of Commons.

Having counselled men and women in a crisis pregnancy, and from my own experience of running the post-abortion course, I think independent counselling on all the options available would be an excellent idea. However, I am not sure that it necessarily follows that numbers of abortions would be greatly reduced if information on psychological risks were included as part of a pre-abortion counselling process.

To a woman in a crisis pregnancy, awareness of the fact that she may suffer lasting psychological or emotional damage by undergoing an abortion (whether it is caused by pre-existing conditions or not) may not make much of a difference to the decision. To her situation, the overriding concern is to get out of the crisis, so she may not be willing to evaluate abortion in terms of a future risk to her mental health, no matter what information on potential risks might be provided. Even if a significant risk were fully established it does not necessarily follow that she would decide not to have an abortion.

However, by understanding that there might be potential psychological or emotional complications, we are forced to ask what drives these potential complications? If we understand that it can be the guilt, the grief and the remorse at the loss of the child that drives the strong feelings that affect so many, we begin to see that abortion cannot be undertaken lightly; that our deepest instincts are to give birth, not to end the life of a child growing in the womb. This changes and deepens our view of abortion.

Dr Vincent Rue, who first connected abortion with symptoms of post-traumatic stress disorder[61], produced an extensive list of criteria for diagnosing post-abortion syndrome. I believe that we have seen all of these symptoms in our post-abortion group including, on one occasion, an individual experiencing hallucinations involving an aborted child.

But that does not necessarily mean I believe people on our course were suffering from a clinically diagnosable post-traumatic stress disorder. Much more widespread was a general experience of depression, anxiety and emotional turmoil caused by the buried sense of grief and loss. For me, the fact that the individuals on the course connected what they were experiencing with the abortion is proof enough of a connection.

For some of those attending our course, what happened after the abortion seemed to be influenced by pre-existing mental health or behavioural issues that perhaps contributed to the abortion in the first place. However, in our (albeit limited) experience, this did not necessarily apply to everyone. As far as we could see, many attending our courses seemed to be normal, well-balanced individuals with seemingly no reason to suspect a pre-existing mental health condition.

The fact, however, that we were able to deal with the problems in the context of the group would seem to indicate some form of link. Certainly the feelings of loss and guilt would not be caused by a pre-existing condition. To me personally Professor Coleman's research rings true, but I do not have any way of judging this objectively.

# Acknowledgements

Bishop Sandy Millar once said that in church life you should be wary of producing a list of people to thank, as invariably someone will be missed off and might take offence.

So many wonderful women have helped organise and lead the Post-Abortion Healing Course at Holy Trinity Brompton since we started in 1993, that it would be difficult for me to produce a complete list going back 20 years. But it is with the women of the counselling teams that my chief thanks must lie, as without their selfless devotion this book would not have been possible. Thank you so much for the countless hours that you spent bringing healing and peace to so many women and men.

Perhaps I could mention by name the team leaders: Nicky-Sue Leonard (now married and ordained Nicky-Sue is The Reverend Nicky-Sue Terry), Caryn Dixon, Terese Williamson and Barbara Salmon, all of whom have led the counselling teams with great vision and passion. Nicky-Sue in particular laid the foundations of this ministry, from our original "Called to Care" course in 1993, and is still involved today. Time after time she battled rush hour traffic at the end of a long working day to meet with us and lead the team, often running three courses a year. Quite simply this would not have happened without her. My thanks also to Margret O'Hara, whose expertise and wisdom enabled us to get started.

When we asked if we could run the course at Holy Trinity Brompton, a number of key leaders were hugely helpful in getting the course off the ground. The consistent support of (now Bishop) Sandy Millar and then Nicky Gumbel, Bob Read and Nicky and Sila Lee, has been a key factor in helping to develop the ministry. I appreciate a post-abortion counselling course must have not seemed an obvious thing to start in 1993, so thank you for your vision and support over the years.

When I started writing this book, a number of key individuals were very encouraging and helpful. My thanks in particular to Lottie Weston, Anna Clarkstone and Olwen Morgan for their encouragement, and to Paul Staley and the many members of CareConfidential who helped with the early manuscripts. My thanks in particular to Jenny Baines who did an excellent job of initially editing the book and to Julia Evans who really helped shape the project.

A great influence in the theology section has been the Revd Sean Doherty, Ethics tutor at St Melitius Thological College. Thank you Sean for your pastoral heart, your wisdom and your common-sense approach to difficult theological issues. My deep gratitude also to Dr Helen Watt of the Anscombe Bioethics Centre for her input and editorial comment.

Lastly there is one person who deserves particular mention: my dear wife Francesca, who has steadfastly backed me in this ministry for twenty years. Thank you for your steady encouragement and support – thank you from the bottom of my heart.

# Notes

[1] Department of Health, 2011. *Abortion Statistics England and Wales: 2010.* London: Department of Health, p.17, Table 4b. See also Appendix VII.

[2] Royal College of Obstetricians and Gynaecologists, 2004. *The Care of Women Requesting Induced Abortion, 2004.* London: Royal College of Obstetricians and Gynaecologists, p.1.

[3] Ensor, J. 2003. Colorado, USA. *Answering the call.* Focus on the Family, p.21.

[4] Biggar, N., 2004. *Aiming to Kill: The Ethics of Suicide and Euthanasia.* London: DLT, ch.3. [I would make an exception in cases such as those where the abortion is taking place to protect the life of the mother, for example, an ectopic pregnancy. In such circumstances, the *intention* behind the abortion is not to end the life of the embryo, but to save the mother's life.]

[5] [We say "innocent life" because the Old Testament (OT) clearly permits and even demands the taking of human life in certain circumstances, such as war and capital punishment. Whether taking life in such circumstances is still permitted by the New Testament (NT) is of course hotly disputed. But it is clear that, if anything, the NT *strengthens* and *intensifies* the OT emphasis on the preciousness of human life. It certainly does not weaken it.]

[6] Wannenwetsch, B., 1998. 'Intrinsically Evil Acts'; or, Why Abortion and Euthanasia cannot be Justified. In: *Ecumenical Ventures in Ethics: Protestants Engage Pope John Paul II's Moral Encyclicals,* eds. Hütter, R. and Dieter, T. Grand Rapids: Eerdmans, pp.185–215.

[7] Stott, J., 1984. *Abortion.* Basingstoke: Marshalls Paperbacks, p.15.

[8] Ibid., p16.

[9] Anon. *The Didache*, p.172.

[10] Coxe, A.C., 1976. *The Ante-Nicene Fathers, Vol. II.* Michigan: Eerdmans, p.147.

[11] YouGov, Plc., 2010. *Arguments on Abortion*. [online] YouGov, Plc. Available at: <http://labs.yougov.co.uk/news/2010/09/22/arguments-abortion/> [Accessed 4 November 2011]. [The poll of 1,636 Catholics from 31 August to 2 September 2010, showed 69% of Catholics agreed that "women should have the right to an abortion" in answer to the question: "Generally speaking, do you think that women should or should not have the right to an abortion?".

[12] Office of National Statistics, 2011. *Statistical Bulletin: Conceptions in England and Wales, 2010*, p.1: 34,633 conceptions to women under 18, a crude rate of 35.5 per 1000 women

[13] Department of Health, 2011. *Abortion Statistics England and Wales: 2010*. London: Department of Health, p.17: 16,460 abortions to those under 18, a crude rate of 16 per 1000 women.

[14] Ibid., p.15–17.

[15] Ibid.

[16] Ibid.

[17] Ibid.

[18] Ibid., p.7. [These figures broadly reflect the general population of the United Kingdom with some slight exceptions, especially among the repeat abortion figures (Table A), which show the overrepresentation of some non-white ethnic groups.]

[19] Ibid., p.15, Table 3a.

[20] Department of Health, 2011. *Abortion Statistics England and Wales: 2010*. London: Department of Health, p.8, paragraph 2.9. [In 2010, 831 abortions were performed under Ground E (congenital deformity) out of a total of 189,574, or 0.43%.]

# NOTES

[21] Bury, L. and Ngo, T., 2009. *"The Condom Broke!" Why do Women in the UK Have Unintended Pregnancies?* London: Marie Stopes International, p.20. [At the time of the unintended pregnancy, 62% of women reported using a contraceptive method.]

[22] Schünmann, C. and Glasier, A., 2006. *Measuring Pregnancy Intention and its Relationship with Contraception Use Among Women Undergoing Therapeutic Abortion.* Association of Reproductive Health Professionals: Contraception Journal, volume 73, issue 5, pp.520–524. [In a study of 316 women in Scotland, 16% were not using contraception, while 44% were using it inconsistently or incorrectly.]

[23] Bury, L. and Ngo, T., 2009. *"The Condom Broke!" Why do Women in the UK Have Unintended Pregnancies?* London: Marie Stopes International, p.8. [Most women who report for abortion counselling say they had no desire to get pregnant, and almost all have information about and access to a variety of contraceptive methods.]

[24] Porter, M., 2009. *It's Time to Think Again About Your Choice of Contraception.* The Times, 26 January. See also: Trussell, J., 2007. Contraceptive Efficacy. In: Hatcher, R.A. et al eds., 2007. *Contraceptive Technology: Nineteenth Revised Edition.* New York, NY: Ardent Media. See also NHS Clinical Knowledge Summaries, 2012. *Contraception – Background information How effective are the various contraceptive methods?* [online] Available at: http://www.cks.nhs.uk/contraception_background_information/effectiveness_of_contraception [Accessed 13 April 2012].

[25] NHS Choices, 2010. *How effective is contraception at preventing pregnancy?* [online] Available at: <http://www.nhs.uk/chq/Pages/825.aspx?CategoryID=117&SubCategoryID=114> [Accessed 04 November 2011]. [Success rate for the combined pill is in excess of 99% "if taken correctly" and 98% for condom use "if used correctly".]

[26] Lewis, C.S., 1977. *The Screwtape Letters: Letters from a Senior to a Junior Devil.* Glasgow: William Collins and Sons, Ltd., p.44.

[27] Bury, L. and Ngo, T., 2009. *"The Condom Broke!" Why do Women in the UK Have Unintended Pregnancies?* London: Marie Stopes International.

[28] Bristow, J., 2008–09. *Abortion Review Special Edition 2*. London: BPAS.

[29] Moran, C., 2007. Abortion: Why it's the Ultimate Motherly Act. *The Times*, 13 April, 2007.

[30] See: Rue, V., 1996. *The Effects of Abortion on Men*. Ethics and Medicine 21 (4): 3–4; Condon, G., and Hazard, D., 2001. *Fatherhood Aborted*. Carol Stream: Tyndale House; and Coyle, C., 1999. *Men and Abortion: A Path to Healing*. Fort Collins: Life Cycle Books; and Jones, K. and Cochrane, L., 1996. *Healing a Father's Heart: a Post-Abortion Bible Study for Men*. Ada, Michigan: Baker Books.

[31] Civil Aviation Authority, 2011. *CAP 382*. London: Civil Aviation Authority.

[32] Los Angeles Times Poll, March 19 1989, question 76. Cited in: Reardon, D., 1999. *Give and Take*. [online] Springfield, Elliot Institute. <http://afterabortion.org/1999/give-and-take/>. [Accessed 4 November 2011].

[33] Bury, L. and Ngo, T., 2009. *"The Condom Broke!" Why do Women in the UK Have Unintended Pregnancies?* London: Marie Stopes International, p.7. ["Reducing the number of unintended pregnancies in the UK is a desirable and achievable goal."]

[34] Reardon, D., 1996. *Making Abortion Rare*. Springfield: Acorn Books, p.152.

[35] Joyce, A., 2000. *"The Only Moral Abortion is My Abortion". When the Anti-Choice Choose*. [online] Available at: <http://mypage.direct.ca/w/writer/anti-tales.html>. [Accessed 5 November 2011].

[36] Office for National Statistics, 2011. *Conceptions in England and Wales 2009*. London: Office for National Statistics.

[37] Lader, D., 2009. *Opinions Survey Report No. 41: Contraception and Sexual Health, 2008–09*. London: Office for National Statistics.

[38] Bury, L. and Ngo, T., 2009. *"The Condom Broke!" Why do Women in the UK Have Unintended Pregnancies?* London: Marie Stopes International.

## NOTES

[39] Trussell, J., 2008. Why Contraception Fails. In: *BPAS, Abortion Review Special Edition 2, Winter 2008–09*. London: BPAS.

[40] Reardon, D., 1995. A Healing Strategy for a Divided Nation. *The Post-Abortion Review 3(1) Winter 1995*. USA: Elliot Institute.

[41] King, M.L., 1963. *Letter from Birmingham Jail (April 1963)* cited in Martin Luther King Day Quotes. [online] Gainesville: University of Florida (Published 1997). Available at <http://grove.ufl.edu/~leo/mlk.html>. [Accessed 10 September 2007].

[42] Black, J., 2004. My Abortion and My Baby, *The Guardian* [online] Available at: <http://www.guardian.co.uk/media/2004/apr/04/channel4.medicineandhealth> [Accessed 18 September 2011].

[43] Povey, D., et al., 2008. *Statistical Bulletin: Homicides, Firearms Offences and Intimate Violence 2006-7 Third Edition*. London: Home Office.

[44] Home Office, 2008. *Statistical Bulletin: Crime in England and Wales 2007–08*. London: Home Office. [The bulletin records 11,648 offences of rape in England and Wales during this period.]

[45] Home Office, 2010. *Statistical Bulletin: Crime in England and Wales 2010–11*. UK: Home Office. [The bulletin records 14,624 offences of rape in England and Wales during this period.]

[46] One large-scale study of in the US estimated a national rape-related pregnancy rate of 5% amongst victims aged 12–45. Of these 32% opted to keep their child, 50% underwent abortion, 6% placed the child for adoption and 12% has miscarriages. Similar figures applied to UK rates would mean 1–2% of all UK abortions were due to rape. see: Holmes M,. Resnick H,. Kilpatrick D,. Best C,.1996: Rape-related pregnancy: estimates and descriptive characteristics from a national sample of women. Charleston USA. Medical University of South Carolina, 1996 Aug; 175(2):320–4.

[47] Reardon, D., Makimaa, J., and Sobie, A., 2010. *Victims and Victors*. Springfield: Acorn Books, p.52.

[48] Ibid., p.63.

[49] Ibid,. p.67.

[50] Holmes M,. Resnick H,. Kilpatrick D,. Best C,. 1996: Rape-related pregnancy: estimates and descriptive characteristics from a national sample of women. Charleston USA. Medical University of South Carolina, 1996 Aug; 175(2):320-4.

[51] Ibid., p.14.

[52] Ibid., p.74.

[53] Ibid., p.95.

[54] Schroeder, D, 2012: My Rape Pregnancy and My Furor Over Social Myths. Washington: Ad Hoc Committee of Women Pregnant By Sexual Assault (WPSA).

[55] Department of Health, 2011. *Abortion Statistics England and Wales: 2010.* London: Department of Health, Table 9. [Congenital malformations were reported as the principal medical condition in nearly half (48%; 1,094) of the 2,290 cases undertaken under Ground E of the Abortion Act. The most commonly reported malformations were of the nervous system (23% of all Ground E cases; 522) and the musculoskeletal system (8%; 181). Chromosomal abnormalities were reported as the principal medical condition for just over a third (36%; 831) of Ground E cases. Down's syndrome was the most commonly reported chromosomal abnormality (21% of all Ground E cases; 482).]

[56] Royal College of Obstetricians and Gynaecologists, 2004. *The Care of Women Requesting Induced Abortion. Evidence-based Clinical Guideline Number 7.* London: Royal College of Obstetricians and Gynaecologists, p.9: 16.9.

[57] Royal College of Obstetricians and Gynaecologists, 2011. *The Care of Women Requesting Induced Abortion. Evidence-based Clinical Guideline Number 7.* London: Royal College of Obstetricians and Gynaecologists, p.45: 5.6.

[58] Coleman, P.K., 2011. Abortion and Mental Health: Quantitative Synthesis and Analysis of Research Published 1995–2009. *The British Journal of Psychiatry (2011)* 199, pp.180–186.

[59] Doughty, S., 2011. How Having an Abortion Can Double your Risk of Mental Health Problems. *Daily Mail*, 3 September, p.8.

## NOTES

[60] See Russo, N.F. and Denious, J.E., 1992. Abortion, Childbearing, and Women's Well-Being. *Professional Psychology: Research and Practice* 23(4), pp.269–280.

[61] Rue, V., 1995. Post-Abortion Syndrome: A Variant of Post-Traumatic Stress Disorder. In Doherty, P., ed.1995 *Post-Abortion Syndrome: Its Wide Ramifications*. Dublin: Four Courts Press.

# WHAT HAPPENS **AFTER AN** ABORTION?

## THE OTHER SIDE OF THE STORY

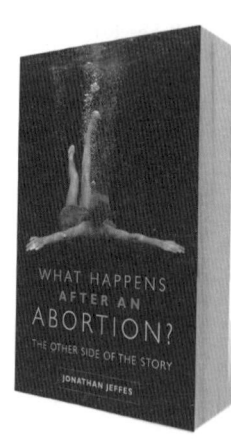

### BY JONATHAN JEFFES

For twenty years Jonathan Jeffes led a post-abortion counselling team at a church in central London. During this time the team counselled over 200 women and around 30 men, many of whom maintained a powerful connection with a past abortion that they were unable to resolve by themselves.

In this dynamic and insightful book, Jonathan reveals the view of abortion through the experience of those who had attended the courses. What do they say about abortion? What to they wish they had known before they made their life-changing decisions?

*"On the courses over the years we have had some really fascinating discussions about life, relationships and the values that lead to an abortion decision. Many of the issues raised are rarely, if ever, discussed in the outside world. In this book I wanted to reflect on some of the deeper issues we have been dealing with and make them available to a wider audience."*

- Why do some women (and men) maintain a powerful connection to a past abortion? What does their experience tell us about the wider issue of abortion?
- What do men think about abortion? What part to they play in the decision making process?
- What do women from our courses who have had an abortion after the tragedy of being made pregnant through rape think about their experience? How did it help them cope with the terrible aftermath of the rape?
- How can women (and men) who maintain an unwelcome connection find healing and restoration?
- What part can the church play in bringing healing and restoration to those in pain from a past abortion?

**ISBN: 978-0-9576513-2-6 | Lean Press Ltd | info@leanpress.co.uk**

# THE POST-ABORTION HEALING COURSE
## *at* Holy Trinity Brompton, London

This course is for women who have been through abortion(s). It is designed for Christians who wish to receive healing and restoration in this area. The course offers a safe place for women to share experiences in a small group setting and to work through the different emotions and consequences following the abortion decision. Confidentiality is always respected.

The course is run over eight sessions, including a full Saturday. Each evening begins with a meal, followed by an interactive talk, discussion/sharing and prayer.

Registration is via email or phone, or by post. You can register with your first name only, if you prefer.

What one woman said about the course: *'I felt very safe and had an opportunity for openness and truth about an issue that was very difficult. Here I felt safe enough to revisit my abortion in an environment that was equipped to handle the consequences effectively and led by individuals who were informed and some of whom had been in a similar position.'*

For details of the next course see: www.htb.org.uk/post-abortion-healing Or contact: courses@htb.org.uk or 020 7052 0323 for further information.